REALITY ORIENTATION FOR THE ELDERLY

REALITY ORIENTATION FOR THE ELDERLY

SECOND EDITION

Sylvester Kohut Jr., Ph.D.
Jeraldine J. Kohut, R.N., M.A.
Joseph J. Fleishman, Ph.D.

MEDICAL ECONOMICS BOOKS
Oradell, New Jersey 07649

Library of Congress Cataloging in Publication Data

Kohut, Sylvester, date
    Reality orientation for the elderly.

    Includes bibliographies.
    1. Gerontology. 2. Aged—Psychology. 3. Aged
—Care and hygiene. I. Kohut, Jeraldine Joanne.
II. Fleishman, Joseph J. III. Title. [DNLM:
1. Aged. 2. Cognition disorders—In old age.
WT 150 R288]
HQ1061.K637   1982   305.2'6   82-8308
ISBN 0-87489-304-6

Design by Douglas Steel

ISBN 0-87489-304-6

Medical Economics Company Inc.
Oradell, New Jersey 07649

Printed in the United States of America

First Edition   1979
Second Edition   1983

To Jeremy John Kohut, age 3,
and his generation

CONTENTS

PUBLISHER'S NOTES

Sylvester Kohut Jr., Ph.D., is Professor and Chairperson, Department of Secondary Education and Foundations, College of Education, Tennessee Technological University, Cookeville. He has served as a program consultant to numerous hospitals, nursing homes, Federal agencies, and educational institutions.

Jeraldine Joanne Kohut, R.N., M.A., N.H.A., is Assistant Professor of Nursing and Director of Continuing Education, School of Nursing, Tennessee Technological University. In collaboration with her husband, she has published widely on the aging process and clinical treatment of the elderly. She is founder and Executive Director of Hospice of Cookeville (Tenn.), Inc. She has served as a nursing-home and hospital administrator/consultant and as a nursing education/geriatric workshop coordinator for numerous institutions.

Joseph J. Fleishman, Ph.D., is Head Clinical Psychologist of the Geriatric Psychology Program at Philadelphia State Hospital. Previously he was a practicing psychologist and gerontologist in Harrisburg, Pa., while a member of the graduate school faculty at the Gerontology Center of the Institute for the Study of Human Development at The Pennsylvania State University—Capitol Campus, Middletown. He is the author of numerous publications and has served as a consultant in the fields of gerontology and psychology.

Joseph F. Rodgers, M.D., who assisted in the preparation of Chapter 4, is Clinical Associate Professor of Medicine at Thomas Jefferson University, Philadelphia. He has maintained a private practice in internal medicine in Philadelphia for over 20 years.

Opless Walker, Pharm.D., author of Chapters 5 and 6, is a Clinical Pharmacologist and Director of Pharmacy Services, Cookeville General Hospital and the Plateau Mental Health Center, Cookeville, Tenn. He has conducted workshops and taught courses in pharmacology for Tennessee Technological University and the University of Tennessee at Knoxville.

"To be seventy years young is sometimes far more cheerful and hopeful than to be forty years old."

—Oliver Wendell Holmes

INTRODUCTION

Throughout this book we stress the importance of touch. An elderly, confused person whose eyesight, hearing, senses of smell and taste, and physical mobility are failing still has two undiminished capacities—the sense of touch and the sense of self. We can think of no finer introduction than these excerpts from "Touch Me!"* by Hazel James.

Touch Me!

I am old. The relentless waves of Time have bruised my body; eroded my bones. Skin that was once firm and elastic has shriveled beneath many summers of flaming suns; has become withered from the caress of icy winds of many winters. My steps are now measured and faltering—from my bed to the wheelchair are agonizing miles. I grope blindly for the glass there on the table beside my bed. My hand touches the plastic bowl of plastic flowers and bitterness rises in my heart. Two years ago this past Mother's Day, they sent them. Two long years ago!

Poker-faced, stern, these strangers minister to my needs. Impersonally, they perform those acts necessary for my survival. To them, I'm not a person. Only a number! Number 54 is tendered medication. Number 54 is bathed, dressed, assisted into her wheelchair. Number 54 is brought her tray. And forgotten!

Touch me, so I'll know I'm still a segment of this vitally alive, pulsating world of human beings and not an inanimate number lying here staring daily at a plastic bowl of plastic flowers. As you give me medication, allow your sturdy fingers to press my trembling ones in reassurance. Such an act will bring back sweet memories of other days; of other hands, clinging, clasping baby hands; hands raised in supplication; pleading for love. Your act will unroll the scroll of Time and, once again, I'll feel tiny arms about my neck, squeezing, clinging. Touch me!

*Copyright © *Crisis,* December 1975. Reprinted with permission of the Crisis Publishing Company, Inc.

xiii

The endless monologues you hear are not senseless ramblings of disoriented minds. They're the heartcries of forsaken souls begging for remembrance. Only the flicker of an eyelash; the remotest trace of a smile! They're wails of love-starved beings, pleading for a crumb of affection. Look at me!

Touch me! The miracle of physical contact will remove the thick crust of disappointment and disillusionment from a heart battered by unkind years. Number 54 will become a person again; a grateful old woman, alive—and thankful! She'll soar beyond her aches and pains; she'll forget plastic flowers in a plastic bowl, and face her day in peace. Trembling hands will grasp each such moment greedily, never letting go. This old, pain-torn body will be revitalized with hope and purpose for when the heart is happy, the soul sings. You'll see! Just touch me!

1

SOCIOLOGY OF AGING

HISTORICAL ANTECEDENTS

The American storyteller and humorist Mark Twain once wrote, "There are statistics, more statistics and damn lies." Contrary to Twain's folksy wisdom, statistical data and actuarial records relating to aging population trends and profiles throughout the United States are not only credible but astonishing. The life expectancy of a person born in 1900 was 47 years, and there were only 3 million persons 65 or older in that year. For a person born today, the life expectancy is over 73 years, and there are now over 25 million "senior citizens." In 1900 pneumonia, tuberculosis, and gastroenteritis were the major causes of death. Today heart disease and cancer are the major causes. Our 25 million elderly represent 12 per cent of the total population. Over 1 million live in institutions, and a significant portion of the institutionalized elderly are incapacitated by disease and degenerative conditions.

People are living much longer. If a person is already 65 years old, his or her average remaining lifetime is 15 years. If you are a descendant of long-lived ancestors, your genes are coded for an even longer life. It helps to be a woman, too. American women live on the average 8 years more than men. Today life expectancy for men is almost 70 years while life expectancy for women is almost 78 years. There are approximately four women for every three men in the 65-and-older category. By 2020, it's predicted there will be over 44 million persons aged 65 years or older and

1

that the elderly will constitute 45 per cent of the entire population of the United States. In view of these enlightening and somewhat startling statistics, it's no wonder there is emerging an awareness of the need to study the aging process and the accompanying problems of the elderly. Our society's interest in self-preservation is reflected in the current boom in the fields of gerontology and geriatrics.

In most industrialized countries, 65 has become the mandatory age for retirement. Why is age 65 the gateway to the so-called golden years? In the late 19th century, Bismarck, the Prussian dictator, while attempting to institute social reforms for his subjects, established 65 as the mandatory retirement age. Retirement was then considered a reward from the state for the worker's many years of toil. The regulation made sense because during that turbulent period in history a person's life expectancy was substantially shorter than it is today, and therefore the actual number of years a worker spent in blissful retirement was few, if any. This made it possible to finance the retirement program without economic strain.

Many industrialized countries with broad technological and Keynesian economic foundations have kept 65 as the mandatory or suggested age of retirement, in the belief that a strong, efficient industrialized society can provide goods and services for all its citizens while "freeing" its elderly to enjoy the better aspects of life. Today, though, it's undeniable that retirement represents, at the least, a mixed blessing. A reward it may be, but the typical accompanying loss of income and prestige leads one to ponder whether substantial punishment isn't associated with retirement. In comparison, the less sophisticated agricultural societies use their human resources as long as possible. Hence their elderly enjoy lifelong respect and financial security. The 1978 legislation raising the minimum mandatory retirement age to 70 will undoubtedly influence the attitudes of unemployed or underemployed younger citizens toward the job-holding elderly.

THE WORSHIP OF YOUTH

A society is a collection of formally and informally related groups organized for mutual survival. The family is the primary unit in our society. It's responsible for child rearing and the social and moral training of our young. It transmits traditions and mores from generation to generation. It assigns roles and status to its members. It provides a series of rewards, reinforcements, and prohibitions that direct our lives in a manner consistent with society's goals and value systems. It's clear that our society places a premium on youth. Exalting youth, we devote many years to the care, nurture, and education of our young.

Alvin Toffler, author of *Future Shock,* submits that we live in a transient society where constant, rapid change is commonplace. An unnecessary side effect of this perpetual motion is the well-known generation gap—or gaps—between the young, the middle-aged, and the old. Because the elderly are neither cherished, like young people, nor productive, like the middle-aged, our society makes them feel obsolete, unwanted burdens.

Each age group has its own balance sheet of credits and debits. Children receive care and nurture, but they have to depend on others to provide it. Adults gain independence, but they must work hard to sustain it. For many old people, though, the modest credits of leisure and the wisdom that only age and experience can bring are far outweighed by the debits: (1) loss of prestige due to retirement, (2) a feeling of aimlessness and uselessness, (3) reduced income, (4) loss of friends who have died, and (5) deteriorating health. The bottom line is self-pity, low self-esteem, and depression.

THE ELDERLY GO ALONG

Why hasn't this state of affairs led to indignant uprisings? Even the Gray Panther organization hasn't attracted a significant number of the elderly, perhaps because they themselves subscribe to conscious and unconscious prejudices against them. The most obvious prejudice arises from the Puritan work ethic: "The Devil finds work for idle hands." It's ironic that some of the strongest proponents of the work ethic are likely to be the elderly. This attitude compounds the problems arising from the idleness they face after forced or voluntary retirement.

The elderly encounter other prejudices. If they do seek work, most retired people can't find it; the response from well-meaning employers is usually a loud, clear No. Studies indicate that, except when life is at stake, persons caring for or working with the elderly don't like their jobs and would prefer working with younger people. The negative stereotypes that contribute to the harsh social climate the elderly encounter are typified by three myths: When people grow old, they lose their mental sharpness, their independence, and their sexuality.

The fastest-growing minority in the United States is the 85-and-over age group. What is an 85-year-old person like today? Born in the Gay Nineties, he or she has witnessed or participated in the Spanish-American War, World War I, World War II, the Korean conflict, and the Vietnam War. He or she has seen the introduction of thousands of inventions and medical and scientific wonders. Many of the elderly are immigrants with roots in the Old World. Many, especially the rural poor, have had little formal schooling. Many are proud, patriotic, and religious and tend to believe in spiritual rather than secular or scientific explanations or solutions to problems. Valuing their privacy and what remains of their independence, they are often shy about discussing severe medical problems as well as everyday aches and pains. Like all people, they need love, friendship, understanding, and respect.

2

PSYCHOLOGICAL ASPECTS OF AGING

As noted in Chapter 1, the elderly have to contend with concrete losses as well as social prejudices. Psychologists generally apply the concept of defense mechanisms to explain how people cope with their problems, including the impositions and aversive qualities of aging. This chapter describes various defense mechanisms and how they may shape personality as well as temper adjustment to the last part of the life cycle. It also describes the psychological characteristics of the aged. The facts about the general mental status of the elderly contrast markedly with the negative stereotype of mental deterioration.

COPING OR DEFENSE MECHANISMS

Anna Freud integrated the ideas regarding defense mechanisms. They may be defined as responses to stress and adversity, largely unconscious in nature, that protect someone from the awareness of threat or anxiety. This concept is rooted largely in psychoanalytic thinking, which emphasizes the influences of early experiences and the unconscious. Although others prefer to explain coping processes from a more cognitive (emphasizing awareness and the rational processes) viewpoint (e.g., Raimy, 1975), it's generally acknowledged that the concept of defense mechanisms provides a natural explanation of the way people cope (Coelho, Hamburg, and Adams, 1974; Greenacre, 1971).

Ten defense mechanisms have been described: repression, denial, projection, intellectualization, rationalization, reaction formation, displacement, fantasy, regression, and identification.

5

Repression, a very basic defense mechanism, means blocking out memories of stressful events. Frequently the memories are of early childhood experiences that threatened psychological security and may include feelings of rejection, anger, sexuality, and dependency.

Denial produces glaring distortions of threatening stimuli. A person may deny his or her assaultive or seductive attitudes or behavior, for example. Needless to say, it is very difficult to communicate with such a person. Denial can be quite upsetting to anyone in contact with a person who uses it.

Projection usually takes two forms; both are partially the results of guilt feelings. One type of projection is illustrated by the case of someone who's long overdue in returning a borrowed item to a friend. Upon seeing the friend, whose expression is noncommittal, the borrower immediately feels she's being judged unfavorably and may start a long and unnecessary explanation of her tardiness. She has projected her guilt onto her friend's facial expression. In the second type of projection, the person attributes his or her feelings to others without any evidence that they actually have those feelings. The distortions associated with this defense can be striking. They sometimes become so strong as to be obvious delusions that have no connection with objective reality.

Intellectualization occurs when a person has developed a rigid (as is the case with all defense mechanisms), dispassionate, affectless (emotionless) way of responding to the world because he fears his own emotions. Such a person will seem isolated from human feelings.

Rationalization is recognizable by frequent alibis and blaming of errors or unpleasant occurrences on objects, events, and other people. The rationalizer handles conflict largely by changing his memory of the circumstances that produced it. The event is still recalled, but in an altered way so that it appears "justified." People excuse their errors in a wide variety of ways, not all of which are convincing. In comparison with the other defense mechanisms, though, rationalization is relatively safe.

Reaction formation is shown by behavior that's the opposite of what is felt. As with intellectualization, there's a rigid style to this behavior. The person appears to be trying to convince all concerned that the behavior in question reflects his true feelings and values. An example might be a person who publicly advocates morality but privately acts immorally or even criminally. "The lady doth protest too much, methinks," from Shakespeare's *Hamlet,* captures the essence of this defense mechanism.

Displacement is an important defense and has gone relatively unnoticed. It means directing one's feelings, such as anger, to an object or person that is not the source of the feelings. The relative lack of attention paid to this defense in the literature may reflect its wide use. So many "hang-ups" and sore spots are handed down from one generation to another that students of personality often fail to acknowledge that the process probably occurs through displacement. For instance, a mother who as a child felt rejected by her parents may convey that rejection to her own children. (Sometimes this displacement is accomplished by the mother's still seeking her parents' approval; this can place pressures on her children and cause them to resent her and feel rejected.) Linden (1974) has pointed out the significance of displacement in the conflict between the generations. Often, he says, these conflicts resurface when circumstances associated with old age bring the parent and child together again under one roof. Many of these feelings have been unresolved since adolescence, and they become surprisingly and frighteningly important when resumption of contact between the generations is anticipated or occurs.

In 1975, the National Institute of Mental Health emphasized the importance of being clear about one's own personal attitudes toward aging and the elderly. There's evidence that training along these lines helps staff who work with the aged treat them humanely and prevent institutionalization syndrome, a form of severe alienation that seems to be fostered in many nursing homes (see Chapter 7). The report cites evidence that this training may prevent staff members from displacing their feelings onto nursing-home residents.

Fantasy is personified in the dreamer or, more accurately, the daydreamer. Singer (1976) has shown the constructive nature of fantasy as an outlet for needs, frustrations, and creativity. The images brought to mind by the fantasy usually reflect the functions it serves. Encouragement of fantasy can frequently relax

7

people and help them express their feelings and ideas. This technique is used by leaders of human relations groups to develop sensitivity and communication among the members (Pfeiffer and Jones, 1974), and it's beginning to be used extensively as an aid to working with aged persons (Weiner, 1976).

Regression means reverting to childish mechanisms of handling stress. It's easy to see why many who work with geriatric patients seem most concerned about the childishness of their patients and quite frequently view aging as a regressive process. Regression is more apt to occur during an acute episode of illness or loss than when life is sailing on an even keel. Because some sick and infirm elderly contribute to the impression that to age is to regress, it's easy to characterize old people as childish. But aging is not a disease, and the aged in general do not regress.

Identification, the 10th defense mechanism, is usually spoken of within the context of early development. A person who takes on the personality qualities of someone he perceives as an aggressor identifies with him: "If you can't beat 'em, join 'em." In the Freudian scheme the aggressor is typically the parent of the opposite sex. Identification, then, has ironic implications; frequently a middle-aged person will note with amazement that he has the very same parental mannerisms or values that in childhood elicited fear, sexual arousal, anger, or feelings of rejection. As the middle-aged offspring acknowledges these resemblances it's sometimes with pride and sometimes with anger. Better understanding between the generations can arise as a result of these insights. "The older I grow, the smarter my father gets" sums it up nicely.

Orthodox Freudians take rather strict positions regarding the role of the unconscious and the structure and function of defenses (e.g., Blau and Berezin, 1975; Goldfarb, 1977; Berezin, 1976) in all individuals. It's also acceptable, however, to view defenses as having a cultural nature, being learned in early childhood and contributing to the ways we communicate and relate to others later in life (e.g., Horney, 1937; Dollard and Miller, 1950). The defenses, which are reinforced by the family—particularly the parents—are more or less adapted to the outside world. This culturally oriented approach makes use of data obtained in experiments on learning.

There's a cause-and-effect relationship between someone's defenses and his attitudes and styles of relating to other people and problems. Some elderly people may appear hysterical in their behavior. An older person may act frantic and become extremely fearful. In all likelihood this is caused by the defense mechanism of denial.

Projection is typically used by a person who sees plots and conspiracies everywhere; such a person is overly suspicious and truly alienated. With the sensory loss and social isolation and loneliness associated with old age today, anyone with a moderate tendency to project is apt to become a nuisance and perhaps even be labeled paranoid.

The "know-it-all" is apt to be using intellectualization. Even though he has a rationale for just about everything, much of what he says may be incorrect or highly personal. "All head and no heart," such a person seems cold and afraid of closeness. His emotions appear to be bottled up and difficult to express.

The "bully" tends to pick on those he sees as his inferiors. His displaced feelings may be expressed in the form of power or social influence or even physically.

"Alibi Ike" has never done anything wrong or made a mistake. Rarely does he admit that he does anything because it feels good; he constructs a rationale that lets him blame something or somebody else.

The "evangelist" uses reaction formation. This person knows the answers and wants to proclaim his knowledge to all the world. In many ways this is an example of the best defense being a good offense.

"Walter Mitty" is a fantasizer. In his own mind he's accomplished many wonderful deeds; only in reality do hard-to-face deficits exist.

Stanley Cath (1976) has demonstrated a concrete, helpful way of thinking about older people and their coping behavior. He has posited an ego-ecological system. Loss is the key problem a person faces in later life, and the body, which frequently has lost energy, health, tone—sometimes a limb or organ—is viewed as an important element of individual integrity. Elderly people undergoing psychotherapy complain very often of these bodily losses or mental deficits. Cath places great emphasis on

9

the therapeutic role of the older person's social and physical environment. The therapist and the people with whom the older person has contact make up his psychosocial milieu; it either encourages or discourages constructive coping. Cath tries to help the elderly client compartmentalize or encapsulate the loss and to respond constructively and, later, enthusiastically to the life that remains. Often diagrams depicting the specific physical reasons for a loss will help. In general, positive personal and bodily imagery contributes to positive coping. Cath observed persons diagnosed as having chronic brain syndrome become very lucid as they gained enthusiasm for life by partaking of a healthful psychosocial environment.

It's encouraging to see reversals in some psychiatric attitudes toward the elderly. The clinical gerontology program at New York University (Blum, 1976) reflects some of the changes in the way psychiatrists view the older person. Traditionally, psychiatrists as much as anyone have gone by the adage that you can't teach an old dog new tricks. The idea that, because infancy and early childhood experiences shape adult personality, only fairly young people can be helped is being modified (Busse and Pfeiffer, 1977). Cath and others see their elderly clients on a continuing basis because they acknowledge the capacity to change and the need for help at any time in life.

The relationship between illness and stress is being increasingly explored. For example, psychosomatic illness is caused by stress manifesting itself in bodily reactions. A great deal has been written about mind-over-matter phenomena (e.g., Whittaker and Fleishman, 1976; Nolen, 1975; Brown, 1975) and the effects of extended stress on health (Stieglitz, 1960; Selye, 1974). At various geriatric centers it's becoming more and more common to find the routine practice of yoga, transcendental meditation, and other forms of training the autonomic nervous system (the system that controls involuntary muscle contractions, such as those of the heart and digestive system). Many psychosomatic complaints sometimes associated with old age, such as high blood pressure, headaches, or ulcers, are now often thought to be reactions to stress that can be modified by natural means or by drugs that calm the adrenergic, or excitatory, actions of the autonomic nervous system. A person who appears to be always in a state of panic or anger, or fight versus flight, as Cannon (1932) originally stated it, is likely to have psychosomatic complaints. As the years accumulate, the toll on his organs becomes more visible.

PSYCHIATRIC PROBLEMS

In addition to showing neurotic behavior, the aged may be psychotic—or they may be well adjusted. While neurotics tend to experience anxiety in their relationships with others and are generally overreactive to life's ups and downs, psychotics tend to lose contact with the stresses of living and can even become dangerous to themselves and/or society. Where clothing is concerned, for example, a neurotic may be overly concerned about his appearance but a psychotic person may go out in the snow partly or completely naked. Such a person is so unresponsive to social and physical cues that he creates personal danger.

At the time of the 1970 Census, approximately 125,000 persons aged 65 or older were confined to psychiatric hospitals, mostly state or county institutions. Another 700,000 were housed in nursing homes, and still another 500,000, in old-age residences—a total of about 1,300,000 institutionalized elderly. Among nursing-home and old-age-home residents, about 80 and 60 per cent, respectively, were diagnosed as moderately to severely mentally disturbed. Thus approximately 9 to 10 million of the institutionalized elderly had significant mental illness in 1970 (Pfeiffer, 1977). This amounts to less than 5 per cent of the approximately 22 million elderly population of the United States. On the basis of other studies, however, Pfeiffer (1977) estimated that as many as *"15 per cent of the elderly population in the United States suffer from significant, substantial, or at least moderate psychopathology."*

Busse and Pfeiffer (1977) have broken down the distribution of the elderly population requiring general mental care and mental institutional care:

Slightly fewer than 1% of persons over age 65 are hospitalized in private or public mental institutions. Of these, roughly half were admitted for psychiatric disorders arising in old age (principally organic brain disease) while the other $\frac{1}{2}$ are individuals admitted for functional psychosis, principally schizophrenia, who have grown old in the hospital. An additional 3% of old people are residing in nursing homes, homes for the aged, and geriatric or chronic disease hospitals; probably about half of these suffer from significant psychiatric disturbances. Combining these data we can say that between 2 and 3% of old people live in institutions as a result of psychiatric illness. . . .

While persons over age 65 make up nearly 30% of patients in public mental hospitals and 11% of those in private psychiatric hospitals, they account for only 2% of the patients seen in psychiatric outpatient clinics. In terms of rates of utilization of outpatient facilities this amounts to only about $\frac{1}{10}$ of 1% of old people receiving outpatient treatment. . . .

The composite picture that emerges . . . is that some 5% of old people living in the community are either psychotic or else have severe psychopathology; when persons with neurotic and personality disorders are added this figure increases to some 15%; and when all degrees of psychiatric impairment are included, ranging from mild to severe, then 25% to nearly 60% of the aged are affected.

It's clear that a large percentage of the elderly experience moderate and sometimes severe emotional problems without seeking or obtaining professional help. To a certain extent this may be due to lack of acceptance of the value of modern psychiatry—a specialty that may be no older than they are. Many may not understand psychiatric approaches to personal and intangible concerns. Likewise, as mentioned earlier, many psychiatrists still are biased against the elderly. This bias ignores the accomplishments and strengths of the present generation of survivors (Curtin, 1972). More concretely, psychiatric care is prohibitively expensive for people on a fixed, limited income. Medicare (medical insurance for the aged) pays for only 190 days total *lifetime* psychiatric hospitalization and only 50 per cent of psychiatric outpatient treatment up to $250 per year after the patient pays the first $100. The inadequacy of this support is clear. For all these reasons, today's elders too often don't receive attention for their emotional problems until they get severe enough to require commitment to a public mental institution.

There is a strong need for outpatient programs and intermediate-care facilities that deal effectively with emotional and adaptive problems not drastic enough to require long-term commitment to a mental institution (Busse and Pfeiffer, 1977). The problems of depression (Linden, 1974; Blum, 1976), regression and psychotic reactions (Cath, 1976; Linden, 1974), and social breakdown syndrome (a form of severe alienation among the elderly in society) (Linden, 1974) are beginning to be studied and treated in their early stages at selected locations. The outpatient center of the Jefferson Medical Center in Philadelphia treats these problems under Dr. Maurice Linden's direction. New York University's Postgraduate Center offers a clinical gerontology program that treats depression and other emotional problems of the aged and trains competent workers to help these people.

Harrisburg (Pennsylvania) Hospital houses a geriatric center that pays particular attention to the complex of behavior in the elderly that results from loss of health, emotional problems, social isolation, and confusion. At present many nursing homes and families are frustrated in their ability to cope with such individuals and are sometimes forced to commit them to state mental institutions or overuse psychotropic (mind-controlling) drugs. Intermediate facilities such as geriatric centers are intended to allow aged persons to return to a more even emotional keel and conduct their lives with dignity.

THE NORMALLY ADJUSTED

Normally adjusted individuals are able to face some very grim realities as long as the circumstances of their lives allow them to remain outgoing and communicative. For many such people, retirement means the opportunity to do the things they've never had time for. It's important to remember that even a well-adjusted individual will use his or her unique, proven coping style in dealing with the losses that will inevitably occur in old age. A certain amount of loneliness and depression is therefore par for the course in normal aging (Taylor, 1974; Busse and Pfeiffer, 1977; Curtin, 1972). Unfortunately, not enough is known (or said) about normal coping processes; psychology has focused in-

13

stead on the negative and attention-getting aspects of behavior. One thing is certain, however: The ability to share feelings is a positive sign of mental health.

THE PSYCHOLOGICAL ASPECTS OF AGING

Birren (1960) edited a handbook on aging that reported a large number of studies on the elderly that showed deficits in sensory processes, psychomotor performance, reaction time, reflex time, and so on, compared with control groups. Only more recently (e.g., Taylor, 1974) have the extent and meaning of these deficits been examined. True, there are sensory-sensivity and sensory-motor decrements, but they're usually tiny—for instance, $\frac{1}{1000}$ of a second in reaction time. While a millisecond may be important to a batter facing Ron Guidry's fast ball or an athlete running the 100-yard dash, for most of us this quickness is not required. Fleishman and Dusek (1972) have shown that time pressures create extra stress that rattles the older person, so it's generally advisable to be patient with an older person—or anyone—if you want him to do his best.

Since Biblical times much has been written about the cognitive stability of older persons, and research (Taylor, 1974; Eisdorfer, 1969) has shown that the elderly are as competent as anybody in making use of long-term memory to arrive at decisions. The fact that they may take a little longer is offset by the greater number of memories they've stored up. Having a wealth of experience to draw on contributes a perspective that a younger person simply can't supply. For practical purposes, therefore, the old can do just about anything as well as their younger counterparts, as long as they're given the time.

SOME GENERAL PERSONALITY QUALITIES

Some general rules of thumb have been suggested concerning the personalities of the old. Old age is usually expected to intensify personal quirks and weaknesses (Curtin, 1972). Taylor (1974) has pointed out that fantasizing on past accomplishments is normal and shouldn't be discouraged. More passive social interaction is also normal (Taylor, 1974); it isn't unusual to find an old person deriving pleasure from observing rather than taking part in group activities.

14

Many of the so-called symptoms of aging are, when analyzed closely, due to the roles imposed on the elderly in the late 20th century. Quite often these symptoms result from social and physical deprivation as well as role expectations. Many old people probably "act their age" simply because they feel expected to do so. It's as if they were saying, "O.K., if you need to see me act this way, I can use it to my benefit."

References

Berezin, M. Paper presented at Continuing Education Conference on Psychodynamics of Aging at New York University Postgraduate Center for Mental Health, New York, 1976.

Birren, J. E., ed. *Handbook of Aging and the Individual.* University of Chicago Press, Chicago, 1960.

Blau, D., and Berezin, M. "Neuroses and Character Disorders." In *Modern Perspectives in the Psychiatry of Old Age* (Howells, J. C., ed.). Bruner-Mazel, New York, 1975.

Blum, J. Paper presented at Continuing Education Conference on Psychodynamics of Aging at New York University Postgraduate Center for Mental Health, New York, 1976.

Brown, B. *New Mind, New Body.* Harper and Row, New York, 1975.

Busse, E., and Pfeiffer, E., eds. *Behavior and Adaptation in Late Life,* 2nd ed. Little, Brown, Boston, 1977.

Cannon, W. B. *The Wisdom of the Body.* Norton, New York, 1932.

Cath, S. Paper presented at Continuing Education Conference on Psychodynamics of Aging at New York University Postgraduate Center for Mental Health, New York, 1976.

Coelho, A.; Hamburg, D.; and Adams, C. *Coping and Adaptation.* Basic Books, New York, 1974.

Curtin, S. *Nobody Ever Died of Old Age.* Little, Brown, Boston, 1972.

Dollard, J., and Miller, N. *Personality and Psychotherapy.* McGraw-Hill, New York, 1950.

Eisdorfer, C. "Intellectual and Cognitive Changes in the Aged." In *Behavior and Adaptation in Late Life* (Busse, E., and Pfeiffer, E., eds.). Little, Brown, Boston, 1969.

Fleishman, J., and Dusek, E. R. "The Equivalence of Alternate Forms of Six Psychometric Measures During Repeated Testing." *Journal of Applied Psychology* 56:186–188, 1972.

Goldfarb, A., "Institutional Care for the Aged." In *Behavior and Adaptation in Late Life* (Busse, E., and Pfeiffer, E., eds.), 2nd ed. Little, Brown, Boston, 1977.

Greenacre, P. *Emotional Growth: Psychoanalytic Studies of the Gifted and a Great Variety of Other Individuals.* International University Press, New York, 1971.

Horney, K. *The Neurotic Personality of Our Time.* Norton, New York, 1937.

Linden, M. Paper presented at Continuing Education Conference on Society and the Aging, Harrisburg Area Community College, Harrisburg, Pa., 1974.

Nolen, W. A. *Healing: A Doctor in Search of a Miracle.* Random House, New York, 1975.

Pfeiffer, E. "Psychopathology and Social Pathology." In *Handbook of the Psychology of Aging* (Birren, J. E., and Schaie, K. W., eds.). Van Nostrand Reinhold, New York, 1977.

Pfeiffer, J. W., and Jones, J. E., eds. *The 1974 Annual Handbook for Group Facilitators.* University Associates, La Jolla, Calif., 1974.

Raimy, V. *Misunderstandings of the Self: Cognitive Psychotherapy and the Misconception Hypothesis.* Jossey-Bass, San Francisco, 1975.

Selye, H. *Stress Without Distress.* Lippincott, Philadelphia, 1974.

Singer, J. *The Inner World of Daydreaming.* Harper and Row, New York, 1976.

Stieglitz, E. "The Personal Challenge of Aging: Biological Changes and Maintenance of Health." In *Aging in Today's Society* (Tibbitts, C., and Donahue, W., eds.). Prentice-Hall, Englewood Cliffs, N.J., 1960.

Taylor, C. Paper presented at Continuing Education Conference on Society and the Aging, Harrisburg Area Community College, Harrisburg, Pa., 1974.

Weiner, I., ed. *Clinical Methods in Psychology.* Wiley-Interscience, New York, 1976.

Whittaker, J., and Fleishman, J. "Biological Foundations of Psychology: Behavior and States of Awareness." In *Introduction to Psychology,* 3rd ed. Saunders, Philadelphia, 1976.

3

THE STEREOTYPE OF DEPENDENCE

One of the common assumptions about aging is that it brings dependence. However, the evidence concerning three reasonably good indicators of dependence—reliance on others for living arrangements, health care, and finances—simply doesn't support this idea.

LIVING ARRANGEMENTS

According to Manley (1969), 75 per cent of the elderly own their own homes. Typically these homes are located in urban areas that have been deserted by younger, white, middle-class families that have moved to the suburbs. These homes are generally strongly built (Manley, 1969) and have served well for raising children. Most of them are fully paid for and therefore are relatively cheap to own. This is important for someone on a limited fixed income. The elderly are deeply rooted in their homes and communities. They know their way around; their neighbors and surroundings are familiar. Many of their friendships are long-lasting and provide a source of mutual help.

Practical problems do arise, however, in maintaining independence—for example, lack of transportation and difficulty in getting up and down stairs. Transportation for the elderly has become an important social issue. Many state programs for the elderly are designed to overcome some of these physical obstacles and make the difference between living at home and entering an institution. Certain state offices of the aging, for instance, operate programs to help meet practical needs arising from incapacities that frequently occur after age 75 and require some form of home care. Strong arguments can be made that these programs significantly lengthen the stay of the elderly in their own homes. This can be especially important to the elderly who have gardens where they can save money by growing food, get exercise, and satisfy their desire for beauty.

Shanas (1969) has presented some informative data on how often older persons communicate with their families. Approximately 80 per cent of the elderly who were interviewed in that study lived within a half-hour's distance from at least one of their children. Two-thirds had seen a child within 24 hours. To a great extent, therefore, the popular image of the isolated elderly is unrealistic. These people are neither isolated nor dependent. It appears that relatives do satisfy many of the social, financial, and affectional needs of the elderly and help them maintain their independence. This idea is definitely supported by data describing the family ties of the institutionalized elderly (see Chapter 7), which suggest that a large percentage are without family (Goldfarb, 1969).

HEALTH—MYTHS AGAIN

As mentioned earlier, it's often the picture of the sick or feeble geriatric patient that causes our misconceptions about aging. The elderly are much healthier, on the whole, than we may think. Estes (1969) reported a comprehensive summary of the distribution of illness among the aged. The aged definitely suffer more chronic conditions, such as high blood pressure, diabetes, and heart disease, but have fewer acute illnesses than younger people, although acute illnesses, when they do occur, are likely to be more severe. Not all chronic illnesses, in fact, depend on age. For example, many younger people have high blood pressure; autopsies of young soldiers during the Vietnam War revealed a high incidence of hardening of the arteries.

The aged also spend less time in bed due to illness than we may think. In 1979 the average hospital stay for persons 65 and over was 10.8 days, compared with 7.2 for the population as a whole (U.S. Bureau of the Census, 1981).

Stieglitz (1960) has an interesting theory about the loss of reserve energy that seems to occur with the wear and tear of age and stress. This reserve—or second wind—is what we draw on when we get tired. Lack of it seems to be what people allude to when they say they're feeling older. Actually it's stress and daily wear and tear (Stieglitz, 1960; Selye, 1974), rather than age, that impair the body's homeostatic (self-stabilizing) processes. Nonetheless we blame "age" for the slowness we sometimes feel. There are many ways to minimize the loss of reserve energy: Regular exercise, good nutrition, meditation, and avoidance of smoking all improve circulation of the blood and contribute to general homeostasis.

FINANCES

In a capitalist country loss of income means loss of social status and presages loss of independence. Therefore loss of income is a very strong and realistic source of fear.

The four main sources of income for the aged, in addition to assistance from children, are Social Security, pensions, salaries and wages, and public welfare programs (Rich and Gilmore, 1972). The true picture doesn't seem as generally gloomy as sometimes described. More than 18 per cent of elderly men and nearly 8 per cent of elderly women are still working, even though they may hold part- instead of full-time jobs (U.S. Bureau of the Census, 1981). There has also been a large increase in the number and value of pensions available to retirees during the last 30 years.

As of March 1980, the mean income of families headed by persons aged 65 or over was $14,727, compared with a mean income for all United States families of $22,376. On the other hand, only 9.1 per cent of families headed by persons 65 or over were below the poverty level, the same percentage as for all United States families. So it's clear that insofar as actual poverty is concerned, the elderly are no worse off than the population in general (U.S. Bureau of the Census, 1981).

There are savings, too. For most elderly people who own their own homes, there are no rent or mortgage payments. With retirement comes extra time for do-it-yourself projects that can provide goods and services that were formerly purchased. These are often swapped informally with friends and neighbors. Finally, gardens can provide food that might ordinarily be bought.

19

The elderly, though sometimes in straitened circumstances, are remarkably proud and independent. The stereotype of financial dependence in old age simply doesn't hold water.

References

Estes, H., Jr. "Health Experience in the Elderly." In *Behavior and Adaptation in Late Life* (Busse, E., and Pfeiffer, E., eds.). Little, Brown, Boston, 1969.

Goldfarb, A. "Institutional Care for the Aged." In *Behavior and Adaptation in Late Life* (Busse, E., and Pfeiffer, E., eds.). Little, Brown, Boston, 1969.

Manley, H. N. Statistic cited in *Behavior and Adaptation in Late Life* (Busse, E., and Pfeiffer, E., eds.). Little, Brown, Boston, 1969.

Rich, T., and Gilmore, A. *Basic Concepts of Aging—A Programmed Manual.* U.S. Government Printing Office, Washington, D.C., 1972.

Selye, H. *Stress Without Distress.* Lippincott, Philadelphia, 1974.

Shanas, E. "Living Arrangements and Housing of Old People." In *Behavior and Adaptation in Late Life* (Busse, E., and Pfeiffer, E., eds.). Little, Brown, Boston, 1969.

Stieglitz, E. "The Personal Challenge of Aging: Biological Changes and Maintenance of Health." In *Aging in Today's Society* (Tibbitts, C., and Donahue, W., eds.). Prentice-Hall, Englewood Cliffs, N.J., 1960.

U.S. Bureau of the Census. *Statistical Abstract of the United States: 1981,* 102d ed. U.S. Government Printing Office, Washington, D.C., 1981.

DISEASES OF THE ELDERLY

The visible changes attributed to old age are easily recognized by society. Most people have a mental image of the stereotypical old person—wrinkled, gray-haired, stoop-shouldered, poorly dressed, and in poor health. But this is inaccurate and does not truly reflect the older American in today's society. Many older persons play tennis, work full-time, dress fashionably, and lead active, independent, healthy lives.

Many gerontologists believe that disease causes aging rather than vice versa. Treatment of underlying pathologic conditions will frequently remove characteristics attributed to old age. For example: The stiffened gait of an elderly arthritis victim can often be greatly improved with proper medical care. And environment, stress levels, and psychological support systems are sometimes as important as medication and diet in promoting optimal health. Nevertheless, there are physiological changes that can affect the later years.

Age-related physical changes occur gradually and are not always visible. They actually begin at conception and are progressive throughout life, with the continuous process of cellular growth, decay, and replacement.

It is unwise to generalize about the physical changes of aging. Each person has individual needs and self-care requisites. The situation of a poor, rural elderly person cannot be compared to that of a wealthy, urban elderly person. They each have different medical and social needs. Consider the following two cases:

Rural Poor: An 81-year-old, undernourished, white female, with poor dentition, productive cough, and shortness of breath. Chest X-ray and laboratory tests confirm tuberculosis. She lives on a farm with her children and five grandchildren. The family is supported entirely by the farm. A recent drought has caused crop failure and poverty. The grandmother shares a bedroom with three grandchildren. There is no money for food, clothing, or medical care.

Urban Upper-Class: An 80-year-old, well-nourished, white female in excellent physical and mental health with negative X-ray and laboratory findings. She lives in a condominium retirement center in Atlanta, five minutes away from her married daughter. The condominium provides in-house nursing service, medical and dental facilities, and daily exercise classes.

These sample cases demonstrate the need for individualized care of the elderly. Whether physical problems occur singly or in combination, the important point to remember is this: Treatment can enable the elderly to return to optimal physical and mental health.

The rest of this chapter will cover some of the more common diseases affecting the elderly population and how those diseases can affect behavior.

CARDIOVASCULAR DISEASES

Diseases associated with deficits in the cardiovascular system are common in the elderly. The aging heart experiences a decrease in cardiac output. The heart rate remains the same or slightly slower at rest in the elderly, but requires more time for recovery after exertion or a stressful episode. With age the heart becomes a poorer pump, the myocardium is more irritable, and the conductive system becomes less than perfect. Blood pressure frequently rises, and the blood vessels may be sclerosed and narrowed. The renal system also suffers from this impaired circulation.

Heart disease is the leading cause of death in the United States today. Contributing factors probably include longer lifespans and more sedentary lives. Cardiovascular disease in the elderly may manifest as heart attack, congestive heart failure, hypertension, stroke, arteriosclerosis, atherosclerosis, or a combination of these.

The elderly patient with any of these disorders may exhibit one or more of the following during acute or rehabilitative phases: social isolation, insomnia, anorexia, depressed and noncompliant behavior, despondency, or even suicide. Inability to work may exacerbate feelings of low self-esteem and depression, as well as contribute to economic hardship. Anxiety over loss of self-image and fear of death are often present.

The most important factor in dealing with the elderly cardiovascular patient is providing adequate rehabilitative programs. Such programs are essential for helping the elderly patient cope with changes in his ability to carry out the routine activities of daily living.

PULMONARY DISEASES

Significant pulmonary deficits are frequently seen in elderly patients. The capacity for adequate breathing may be diminished; the efficiency of the entire respiratory cycle may be decreased. Without adequate amounts of oxygen, many bodily functions are compromised. These deficits are caused not only by biological aging processes, but also by smoking and prolonged exposure to polluted air in urban or occupational environments.

Pulmonary diseases common to older persons include emphysema and pulmonary fibrosis. Single entities or a combination of diseases may be present. Chronic obstructive pulmonary disease (COPD) may result from a number of different conditions. COPD is ranked second only to heart disease as a cause of death or disability in the United States. It is increasing at alarming rates due, at least in part, to longer life-spans, better detection, and improved survival of patients with the acute conditions that cause it.

Behavioral characteristics associated with pulmonary diseases may include: dependence due to inability to perform activities of daily living, depression, excitability, and anxiousness. When oxygen intake is decreased, confusion, weakness, and irritability can be demonstrated.

MALNUTRITION

A substantial portion of elderly persons in the United States suffer from malnutrition. Lack of desire to eat, poor income, loneliness, and poor dentition are all contributing factors. (See Chapter 6 for a more detailed discussion of nutrition in the elderly.)

When adequate amounts of vitamins and minerals are not supplied, the cardiovascular, skeletal, and muscular systems can be affected. Behavioral manifestations may include listlessness, weakness, irritability, and depression. Elderly people living alone should be encouraged to eat with family or friends, or in other available communal situations.

CANCER

Cancer affects all age groups, but is more common in older persons. Most cancer deaths occur over the age of 55. This may be because older persons have been exposed to carcinogens for longer periods of time. Cancer is more common in urban dwellers than rural dwellers and in males than females. Early detection remarkably improves survival rates in certain cancers.

The basic cancer treatment modalities are the same for patients of every age: surgical intervention, chemotherapy, and radiation. The type of cancer, the patient's current physical status, and other details of each case determine the choice of therapy for a given patient.

A cancer diagnosis is devastating. To most people, cancer still connotes terminal disease, mutilation, and death. Cancer patients may have to cope with changes in body image, weakness, anorexia, or sensory deprivation in intensive-care units. Stress and lowered self-esteem are often apparent. Listlessness, loneliness, and feelings of isolation frequently follow a cancer diagnosis. Anticipatory grieving can occur, especially if metastasis has been diagnosed. Shock, fear, denial, anger, and acceptance may appear in stages.

The care-giver must pay particular attention to how the patient is coping, try to understand and encourage his coping mechanisms, and, in addition, provide support for the patient and his family.

PSYCHOLOGICAL DISORDERS

Most psychopathology in later life is precipitated by the crises of aging—biological, psychological, or social. These disorders are usually accompanied by feelings of loss, inferiority, and depression. (See Chapter 2 for a more complete discussion of psychopathology and aging.) A major difficulty is that many persons accept these disorders as an inevitable part of the aging process, and do not seek help until acute or severe problems appear.

Symptoms of psychological disorders in general might include: withdrawal from activity, lack of interest in physical appearance, insomnia, anorexia, constipation or diarrhea, suspiciousness, hostility, delusions, and feelings of inferiority.

BONE AND JOINT DISEASES

One of the most frequent accompaniments of aging is increasing brittleness and fragility of the bones. Osteoporosis affects one out of every three women and one out of every five men over the age of 50.

In osteoporosis, the bones become weaker and thinner due to an interference in the bone rebuilding process. Backache and other skeletal pain are common symptoms. Patients can be very irritable due to constant, nagging pain, may tire easily, feel weak and shaky when standing, and become extremely apprehensive about falling. Depression may result from inability to perform daily activities due to pain and the immobility it causes. Osteoporosis is treated with a diet high in calcium, phosphorus, protein, and vitamin D, and exercise.

Osteoarthritis can occur in any joint, but is most common in the knees, hips, and spine. Arthritis results from degeneration of the cartilage that lines the joints. It is treated with a diet high in protein, vitamins A, B, C, and E, exercise to keep the joints mobile, and medication prescribed according to the severity and the degenerative process involved.

Arthritic patients may show signs of depression resulting from pain and inability to carry out daily activities. Immobility may cause loss of interest in self and inability to cope with life patterns. Sadness and self-pity can become paramount in the self-concept.

Arthritis is common in the elderly, and can be devastating. It may totally change a person's ability to function in society, especially without a support system.

DIABETES

Diabetes mellitus is one of the most common endocrine diseases in the United States, affecting several million people. It is more common in those who have relatives with the disease, and in overweight persons over the age of 40. Longer life-spans, greater public awareness, and excellent patient education programs via the family practitioner have contributed to the increase in reported cases of diabetes.

Diabetic complications may significantly affect the lives of elderly patients. Diabetes is a leading cause of blindness in the United States today. Chronic kidney disorders, increased susceptibility to infections, peripheral neuropathy, and vascular degeneration sometimes causing loss of limbs are other common complications.

Behavioral changes revolve around the patient's loss of control of his environment. The frightening experience of losing a limb or the panic of being in a world of darkness can cause fear, frustration, depression, anxiety, and loss of self-concept. Education and counseling are critical in helping the patient regain control of his life situation—a paramount issue for the elderly.

Every person past the age of 50 should have a complete physical examination at least annually. The checkup should be multiphasic and include screening for blood pressure, tuberculosis, glaucoma, oral and breast cancer, blood sugar, and hearing deficiencies.

With proper nutrition and exercise, and with careful evaluation and treatment when necessary, the elderly can be helped to maintain optimal health and independence.

References

Brink, T.L. *Geriatric Psychotherapy.* Human Sciences Press, New York, 1979.

Butler, R.N. Paper presented at National Institute on Aging, Speakers Forum, Washington, D.C., 1976.

Cole, W., and Harris, D. *The Elderly in America.* Allyn and Bacon, Boston, 1977.

Ebersole, P., and Hess, P. *Toward Healthy Aging.* C.V. Mosby, St. Louis, 1981.

5

DRUG THERAPY IN THE ELDERLY

MULTIPLE MEDICATIONS

Elderly persons are frequently treated for more than one chronic condition simultaneously, sometimes by different physicians. It is essential that physicians and pharmacists instruct elderly patients to keep complete lists of all medications being taken at any given time, plus records of drugs taken during the previous 12 months, since the effects of some drugs with long half-lives may persist in the body long after the last dose is taken. This information will give the physician a more complete picture of the elderly patient's health status, aid in diagnosis and treatment, and help prevent harmful drug interactions.

Drugs should be used with more than usual care in the elderly. Altered renal or hepatic function, erratic gastric absorption, metabolic changes, and chronic illnesses may affect the action of drugs in the body. Medications should be prescribed only when potential benefits to the patient outweigh potential harmful effects.

PATIENT COMPLIANCE PROBLEMS

It seems ironic that a patient will make the effort to see a doctor and have a prescription filled, but neither follow the doctor's advice nor take the medication as directed. Yet such compliance problems are not at all unusual.

There are many reasons for noncompliance—confusion over complicated multiple-drug regimens, inability to clearly read prescription labels, forgetfulness, dissatisfaction with treatment

27

received, drug side effects, cost, and so on. Some patients simply cannot swallow capsules, while others insist that tablets stick in their throats. A patient may declare that the tablet form of a medication is much more effective than the capsule form of the same drug. Patients have been known to spit out medications given in any form other than liquid. One elderly institutionalized patient bragged that no medicine ever tasted bad to him; he could "swallow any liquid." Yet, the thought of taking a solid dosage form would make him gag.

In some instances, patients may actually have legitimate complaints. For example, uncoated tablets, such as some aspirin and ascorbic acid preparations, may get stuck in the throat, producing a choking syndrome. It is very important for pharmacists, physicians, and other health professionals to warn patients against taking tablets or capsules too large for their swallowing ability. Other guidelines include:

- Solid dosage forms should never be taken without a liquid. Pills should never be "dry-mouthed."
- Some liquid should be taken first, to wet the throat before the pill is swallowed.
- The patient should inhale and hold the breath in before swallowing a tablet or capsule. This will aid in the removal of the pill if it gets stuck in the throat area. The extra air in the lungs will be a force available if needed.
- In many cases, capsules that are difficult to swallow may be opened and the contents taken as a powder. However, it is usually advisable not to open capsules containing timed-release pellets, since it is difficult to ensure that contents will not be crushed or chewed.
- Some tablets may be crushed or broken if needed to make them easier to swallow. *CAUTION:* Timed-release tablets should never be crushed or broken. This may allow too much drug to reach the circulation at one time. Other tablets that should not be crushed include enteric-coated tablets and uncoated tablets designed to be dissolved in the mouth.
- Liquid forms should be used, if possible, when swallowing is a problem. See Appendix 6 for information on availability of liquid formulations and advisability of opening capsules or crushing tablets for about 200 common drugs.

- Patients should never take any medication while laughing or talking. Full attention should be directed to swallowing.
- Water (or another liquid) should always be taken before swallowing viscous or irritating liquids such as cough syrups or citric acid preparations. Medications of this type may produce coughing spasms that can be harmful, especially to patients with histories of heart attack or convulsions. A little water taken first may help suppress the coughing reflex.

NONPRESCRIPTION DRUGS

Most of the drugs in the typical home medicine cabinet are nonprescription or over-the-counter (O.T.C.) drugs. Self-treatment with O.T.C. drugs tends to be frequent among the elderly. There are a number of reasons for this. Many elderly persons with limited incomes cannot afford physicians' or emergency room fees. Medicaid and Medicare can often help, but certain Federal regulations can sometimes make it difficult for patients to receive all the medical help they feel they need. Elderly patients cannot always arrange for office visits at convenient times, or may have difficulty arranging transportation. And many people simply take the path of least resistance.

It is estimated that expenditures for O.T.C. drugs increase with age. Persons over age 65 in this country spend one-third of their medication dollar on O.T.C. drugs. Studies have shown that the elderly frequently use nonprescription analgesics, antacids, cough and cold preparations, laxatives, and vitamins, and most often, do not consult physicians about their use.

O.T.C. ANALGESICS

Many elderly people have very low pain thresholds and may tend to over-use O.T.C. analgesics. Advertising claims often reinforce this behavior. Yet indiscriminate use can lead to toxicity, to which the elderly seem especially prone.

Here's an example of the kind of risk the indiscriminate O.T.C. user may be taking: For years, phenacetin was a common ingredient in many O.T.C. analgesic products. Eventually it was linked with a risk of kidney damage. Phenacetin has now been voluntarily dropped from most products that once contained it (and products that still contain it must carry warning labels), but millions of older people took many tons of the chemical before the dangers were known. Companies are now advertising phenacetin-free products, and *aspirin, acetaminophen,* and *caffeine* dominate the O.T.C. analgesic market.

Indiscriminate use of even phenacetin-free analgesics may lead to analgesic nephropathy and associated hypertension. Females are affected three times as often as males, and the patients most at risk are those who regularly use analgesics for chronic pain, such as from backaches, arthritis, or headaches.

Aspirin is the most frequently used nonprescription analgesic. It is currently estimated that over 200 O.T.C. preparations contain it. Some trade names and advertisements for aspirin-containing products give no indication that aspirin is an ingredient. This can easily cause confusion for an elderly person who wishes to avoid aspirin and is not in the habit of reading product labels. For example, an elderly woman in New Orleans, who had been instructed by her physician to avoid aspirin, declared, "I don't take aspirin, I take Anacin instead!" (Though Anacin-3 is aspirin-free, aspirin is the main ingredient in regular Anacin.)

Though aspirin is by no means physically addicting, psychological dependency has occurred. A 72-year-old Boston nursing-home resident, for example, took two aspirin every night at bedtime, insisting he could not get to sleep without it. Yet aspirin has no sedative properties.

As an analgesic, aspirin ranks high. Its antipyretic and anti-inflammatory properties further increase its usefulness. But there are potential problems. Hypersensitivity reactions, gastrointestinal blood loss, and drug interactions, especially with oral anticoagulants and uricosuric agents, are possible. See the table on the next page for some of the more significant drug interactions involving salicylates.

Symptoms of overdose or toxicity appear at lower doses in the elderly than in younger people. Irritability, confusion, and deafness may appear quickly. Dyspepsia occurs in a small number of patients, especially in those with rheumatoid arthritis. Salicylates may cause decreased sodium and chloride excretion, which can lead to edema. This possibility is of special concern to patients on low-sodium diets or with congestive heart failure.

DRUG INTERACTIONS INVOLVING SALICYLATES	
DRUG	EFFECT WITH SALICYLATE
Alkalinizers, urinary	Increased excretion and decreased effect of salicylates
Aminosalicylic acid (PAS)	Increased possibility of salicylate toxicity
Anticoagulants	Enhanced anticoagulant effect
Corticosteroids	Increased danger of gastrointestinal ulceration
Methotrexate	Increased methotrexate toxicity
Phenobarbital	Decreased effect of salicylates due to enzyme induction
Phenylbutazone	Increased danger of gastrointestinal ulceration
Phenytoin	Increased phenytoin effect
Probenecid	Antagonism of the uricosuric effect of probenecid
Sulfinpyrazone	Antagonism of the uricosuric effect of sulfinpyrazone
Sulfonylureas	Enhanced hypoglycemic effect of the sulfonylureas

Chronic use of aspirin or any salicylate may cause a decrease in iron reserves due to blood loss associated with gastrointestinal irritation. Since older people are frequently suffering from iron-deficiency anemia anyway, this can complicate an existing problem. Patients with anemia should avoid aspirin if possible. One to four aspirin tablets (5 grains each) can prolong bleeding time by several minutes. Intake of nine 5-grain tablets a day can cause as much as 6 ml. of blood loss daily. Fifteen per cent of patients lose 10 ml., or 2 teaspoonfuls daily. Chronic aspirin use has been associated with chronic ulceration. This in turn creates a need for another product often over-used by the elderly—*antacids.*

The following case is not unusual: A Philadelphia patient complained of pain when swallowing as well as pain in the lower intestinal tract. She was given a complete physical examination by a gastroenterologist, who found an irritated esophagus and small intestine. The patient's history included long-term daily intake of an effervescent aspirin-containing product. Such

31

long-term use was contrary to the instructions on the label. The patient was advised to stop taking aspirin products, and her condition improved.

Even though aspirin is still the most-used drug in America, acetaminophen is quickly becoming a popular substitute when analgesic and/or antipyretic actions are needed. But acetaminophen is not an anti-inflammatory, as aspirin is, and is not as effective for rheumatoid arthritis. Acetaminophen has some advantages: It will not produce gastric irritation or erosion, as aspirin can, and it does not cause occult blood loss.

Although acetaminophen is not effective in severe pain, its effect may be enhanced by increasing the dosage to 1,000 mg. Doses larger than that do not enhance analgesia but do increase the toxicity of acetaminophen. High doses can be extremely toxic and sometimes fatal. In Great Britain, more than 5,000 persons are admitted to hospitals each year due to acetaminophen overdosage. Fifty to 100 of those patients die. Acetaminophen poisoning is also becoming common in this country.

Toxic doses can injure the liver, kidneys, heart, and central nervous system. The drug is oxidized to toxic metabolites, and liver damage develops within hours of ingestion (of toxic doses), after the detoxifying agent glutathione has been depleted. In known acetaminophen overdosage, induction of vomiting may help only if it is done promptly, since the drug is rapidly absorbed. Only 30 minutes after 1 gm. of acetaminophen is taken, 10 gm. of charcoal will reduce total absorption only 30 per cent. In fatal cases, the blood may be chocolate-colored, and degenerative changes may be found in the liver and kidneys.

ANTACIDS

Twenty per cent of Americans suffer from acid indigestion or "heartburn," and the majority of those sufferers treat themselves with O.T.C. antacids, sometimes indiscriminately.

Many available antacid products are safe and effective when used as directed. But abuse of these products is not uncommon. For example, one 72-year-old St. Louis area man regularly drank antacid right out of the bottle without measuring the doses. He was self-treating what he believed to be ulcers. He complained of being "very nervous" and worried a great deal about unlikely and inappropriate things—such as his town running out of water during the summer, and the water pipes freezing in the mobile trailer in which he no longer lived. In short, his problems were mostly imagined. But the stress in his life caused many physiological problems including "heartburn." This patient bought antacids by the case and relied on them daily. He was one example out of the thousands who spend $500 million on antacids in the United States every year.

Many elderly people rely on sodium bicarbonate (baking soda) as an antacid. It cannot be denied that sodium bicarbonate does an excellent job of neutralizing excess acid (as well as needed acid). But it causes acid-rebound: Acid production is greater after taking sodium bicarbonate than it was before. There is also some systemic absorption that can upset the acid-base balance, causing alkalosis. For these reasons, sodium bicarbonate should be reserved for occasional use only.

The following case illustrates how harmful the over-use of sodium bicarbonate can be: A 76-year-old Seattle man habitually took a teaspoonful of baking soda every night at bedtime. During the night he would get up frequently to take further doses to relieve his upset stomach. The patient died at 78 from massive ulcerations of the stomach and problems associated with disturbed acid-base balance.

Anyone who takes any type of antacid should heed the warnings found on the labels of most major brands. The warnings may include:

- Do not take more than [specified dose] in a 24-hour period or use for longer than two weeks except under the advice and supervision of a physician. (A patient who needs antacids for longer periods may actually have a pathological condition requiring diagnosis and treatment by a physician.)
- Do not use this product if you have kidney disease except under the advice and supervision of a physician. (O.T.C. antacids may contain more than 25 mEq. of potassium per daily dosage.)
- Do not use this product if you are on a sodium-restricted diet, except under the advice and supervision of a physician. (Many products contain more than 5 mEq. of sodium per daily dosage.)

Antacids may have laxative or constipating effects that can add to existing bowel disturbances so common among the elderly. Labels should be checked carefully. Products found to have laxative effects in greater than 5 per cent of patients must carry the warning: "may have a laxative effect." Products causing constipation in greater than 5 per cent must warn: "may cause constipation." A patient who has a problem with a particular product may be better off trying an alternative.

The most significant antacid drug interaction involves tetracycline. When antacid comes in contact with free tetracycline in the intestine, the absorption of tetracycline can be decreased by 50–100 per cent, significantly interfering with the intended antibiotic therapy. Antacids should generally be avoided during tetracycline therapy; many antacid product labels carry warnings to that effect.

The taste factor is very important in patient compliance with antacid therapy, and personal preference may be followed when possible. Other helpful guidelines for antacid therapy include the following:

- Liquid and powder forms are more effective than tablets because dispersion in the stomach is faster and surface area is greater. One tablespoonful of liquid antacid is as effective as three tablets.
- Tablets generally taste better than liquids due to the decreased surface area.
- If tablets are used, they should be thoroughly chewed or dissolved in the mouth before swallowing. Tablets swallowed whole are much less effective in neutralizing acid.

COUGH AND COLD PREPARATIONS

There is general agreement that O.T.C. cough and cold remedies can be effective in relieving the symptoms of the common cold. But they are not without risk.

Cold preparations containing *antihistamines* can cause drowsiness and have been implicated in car accidents.

Preparations containing *anticholinergics,* such as the belladonna alkaloids, may cause excessively dry mouth, constipation, insomnia, excitement, confusion, rapid pulse, or blurred vision. If any of these side effects appear, the medication should be discontinued. Patients with asthma, prostate enlargement, or angle-closure glaucoma should avoid anticholinergics. Patients already taking drugs with anticholinergic effects, such as phenothiazines, antiparkinsonism drugs, and tricyclic antidepressants, are much more likely to develop side effects when O.T.C. anticholinergics are added.

Preparations containing *sympathomimetic amines,* which are used for their bronchodilating and decongestant properties, may induce dizziness, nervousness, and insomnia in elderly persons. Diabetics taking these preparations may require insulin dosage adjustments.

Many *cough preparations* contain large amounts of sugar and are contraindicated in diabetes. Cough medicines should *not* be used for chronic problems, such as asthma or emphysema, in which cough relief may cause harmful retention of respiratory secretions.

The side effects mentioned above can occur at normal, recommended doses. Problems are even more likely in people who drink right from cough syrup bottles without measuring doses, or who otherwise exceed recommended limits.

LAXATIVES

Laxatives are one of the most used and abused classes of drugs, especially among the elderly. They cannot be considered totally safe or harmless. They are habit-forming drugs and are one of the most frequent *causes* of constipation.

Stimulant laxatives produce bowel evacuation by artificial over-stimulation of the intestinal tract. This keeps the bowel muscles from doing their job. With prolonged laxative use, natural peristalsis can diminish, as bowel muscles become lazy and inactive, and begin to atrophy. Chronic constipation results. This problem has been known to have significant effects on the behavior of elderly patients.

Other types of laxatives are less likely to cause dependence, and should be given preference when possible. Bulk-forming laxatives, such as the psyllium-containing preparations, work by expanding during contact with water. The intestinal tract responds in a natural manner to the increased pressure they cause. This allows for a natural bowel movement without harm to the tone of the bowels. Nevertheless, no laxative is right for every situation. Careful evaluation of the individual patient is necessary to select the best laxative.

Many people believe that a bowel movement is necessary for proper health. They must be educated regarding normal bowel frequency: It can vary from three times daily to three times weekly.

The following case illustrates how a pattern of laxative abuse can develop: A 72-year-old woman experienced an attack of diarrhea and took an O.T.C. antidiarrheal (kaolin/pectin) product. Twenty-four hours later, she decided to take some milk of magnesia because she felt constipated and had not yet had a bowel movement that day. Such excessive concern over bowel habits can lead to irrational behavior and self-preoccupation, as well as actual physical harm.

Most experts agree that laxatives are indicated only in unusual circumstances. Valid indications may include:
• Necessity to avoid straining.
• Coronary artery disease.
• Aortic aneurysm.
• Cerebrovascular accident.
• Partial or complete loss of rectal reflex.
• Altered bowel motility caused by drug therapy.
• Atrophied abdominal and perineal muscles.
• Diminished food intake.

If none of the above are present, then laxative use should be carefully evaluated, especially if any of the following are present: fecal incontinence, mental disturbance, intestinal obstruction, urine retention, or rectal bleeding.

The goal of every elderly person should be to keep the intestinal tract in as good condition and tone as possible. This is best accomplished with a diet high in fiber and relatively low in meat, adequate daily fluid intake, and regular exercise. Intestinal tone is also aided by avoiding laxative use unless it is absolutely necessary.

Nonprescription medications can often enhance an elderly person's comfort and well-being. But they should be used with caution—not only because of possible side effects or toxicity, but also because they can sometimes mask the symptoms of a serious underlying disorder requiring more aggressive treatment by a physician. Because of the special problems of the elderly, that advice is probably more important for them than for any other age group.

References

United States Department of Health, Education and Welfare. *Long-term care facility improvement campaign.* DHEW Publ. No. (OS) 76-50050. U.S. Government Printing Office, Washington, D.C., 1976.

Walker, Opless. Unpublished observations, 1969–1982.

6

NUTRITION IN THE ELDERLY

Nutrition has a major role in the proper health care of the elderly. Too many older people rely exclusively on synthetic or natural medicines to cure their aches and pains, while overlooking the importance of proper diet, vitamin supplements, and adequate physical exercise.

Malnutrition is a frequent contributor to morbidity and mortality in the elderly. It decreases immunocompetence, rendering patients much more susceptible to infection and disease. Malnourished institutionalized patients are highly susceptible to non-healing bedsores or decubitus ulcers.

FACTORS CONTRIBUTING TO MALNUTRITION

The prevalence of malnutrition in the elderly can be attributed to a number of factors, including:

Chronic drug use. Diuretics may increase the need for potassium, magnesium, and zinc. Aspirin in large doses, as may be prescribed for rheumatoid arthritis, increases the need for vitamin C. Since drugs may also dull the appetite, the drug regimen should be carefully reviewed in cases of suspected malnutrition.

Illness. Chronic ailments such as heart conditions, digestive tract problems, poor teeth or gums, and a wide range of dietary restrictions can cause severe nutritional problems. In addition, emotional problems may cause diminished appetite, resulting in poor nutrition.

Ignorance of proper diet. Many older people just don't know how and what to eat. Ongoing educational programs are needed—both in institutions and for the general public. Americans have become "fast-food" junkies, and many people, including the elderly, are guilty of forsaking well-balanced meals. Excessive intake of alcoholic beverages or soft drinks can also interfere with proper nutrition by diminishing the desire for food.

Financial and logistical problems. Because of fixed, limited incomes, many elderly people can't afford proper, well-balanced diets. In isolated rural communities, many don't have adequate transportation to and from grocery stores. Urban dwellers living alone are often afraid to venture out of their immediate neighborhoods to get to large supermarkets, relying instead on nearby convenience markets and frozen or precooked meals.

Reduced sense of taste and smell. Very old persons are often less conscious of hunger because of reduced sensitivity to taste and smell. This can lead to reduced stomach activity. Between the ages of 30 and 75, the reduction in taste buds or capacity for tasting may be as much as 60 per cent.

Secondary malnutrition. Poor digestive processes are not uncommon in the elderly. Certain disorders of the esophagus, including spasms, cancer, hiatal hernia, or diverticulitis, may retard the passage of food to the stomach. Hypermotility of the stomach and hypomotility of the intestinal tract are common. Hypoactive salivary glands may diminish the digestive process. Digestive enzyme activity may be lacking in the stomach, pancreas, and small intestine. The liver and biliary system may be producing less bile. All these factors can lead to stomach problems and abdominal pain.

Atherosclerosis and circulatory diseases may interfere with the proper distribution of nutrients to body cells. Because of loss of storage cells, foods may provide only short-term benefit. Metabolism, especially of minerals and electrolytes, may be altered due to tissue changes. With aging, increased loss of muscle and kidney function can contribute to increased protein loss.

OBESITY

Over 50 per cent of the American population is overweight to some extent. Our tendency to lead sedentary lives contributes to this dubious distinction.

The following is a somewhat extreme example of an all-too-common syndrome: A 70-year-old woman living in Los Angeles cooked continuously, using saturated fat as seasoning. Her specialties were cakes and pies with plenty of sugar. She usually ate as much as she served to her friends and relatives, until she tipped the scales at 290 pounds. Her obesity, coupled with her sedentary life, eventually caused her "early" death. Her death was directly attributed to her lifestyle and bad habits, which resulted in a state of ultimate deterioration.

Obesity is actually a type of malnutrition. Six of the 10 leading causes of death in the United States—heart disease, cancer, stroke, diabetes, arteriosclerosis, and cirrhosis of the liver—are linked directly to dietary habits, primarily the overconsumption of *saturated fats, cholesterol, sugar, salt,* and *alcohol.*

Since 1909, fat consumption has increased over 25 per cent. Fat now accounts for almost 42 per cent of caloric intake in the average American diet. Caloric intake from carbohydrates has decreased 9 per cent, but much of it comes from sugar and alcohol. Alcohol, fats, and sugar are low in vitamins and minerals, and malnutrition can result from an overconsumption of them.

DIETARY RECOMMENDATIONS

Cholesterol consumption should not exceed 300 mg. per day. Since a medium-size egg contains approximately 300 mg. of cholesterol, this recommendation presents a real challenge to many people.

It is estimated that Americans consume 85 per cent more salt than is needed in their daily diets. Recommended total daily intake is 3 gm., approximately the amount in two hot dogs. New habits must be learned—for example, it is not necessary to add salt to food before, during, or after cooking.

Other helpful hints for healthful dining include:
- Fruits and vegetables, especially those with high fiber content, should be an important part of the daily diet.
- More poultry and fish should be added to the diet, and consumption of other types of meat curtailed.
- Nonfat milk should be substituted for whole milk. But note that low-fat milk contains much higher concentrations of sodium than whole milk.

41

- Alcoholic beverages should be limited.
- Refined sugar should be limited or avoided.
- Cholesterol should be reduced; eggs should be limited.
- Baked or broiled foods should be favored over foods that are fried.
- Salt should be limited.
- Foods containing additives (preservatives, coloring agents, etc.) should be avoided or drastically limited.

Caloric intake should be spaced evenly throughout the day. A person who eats no breakfast and very little lunch can still gain weight. An excessive intake of carbohydrates at the evening meal can't be converted to energy at one time and will, instead, be converted in the liver to fat, producing weight gain. This is why the after-dinner stroll is a good practice, especially when the meal is high in carbohydrates.

AGE-RELATED CHANGES

Although the needs of the elderly may not be age-related, it can be shown that:

- A 75-year-old man has a metabolic rate approximately 15 per cent lower than a 30-year-old man.
- Total body water decreases by about 18 per cent from age 30 to age 75.
- The proportion of body fat to body weight may increase with age. Increase of body fat with a proportionate decrease in body lean is undesirable.
- In men, energy expenditure decreases 21 per cent between age 20 and age 74, and 31 per cent between age 75 and age 99.
- Caloric requirements are decreased in the elderly because of lower basal metabolism and decreased physical activity.
- For many reasons, appetite is often diminished in very old persons, leading to reduced intake of nutrients.

Throughout the United States today, there is a growing awareness of good health practices, especially among the young. Our fascination with jogging, walking, aerobics, health clubs, organic gardening, and so on, can have positive health effects. Unfortunately, these trends have not had a great effect on the elderly, especially the institutionalized elderly.

NUTRITIONAL NEEDS

The Food and Nutrition Board of the National Academy of Sciences has provided Recommended Daily Dietary Allowances (RDA) for certain vitamins and minerals based on current research data. The recommendations for men and women over age 50 are reproduced in the accompanying table.

RECOMMENDED DAILY DIETARY ALLOWANCES		
	Males Over Age 50	Females Over Age 50
FAT-SOLUBLE VITAMINS		
Vitamin A (retinol equivalents)[1]	1,000 R.E.	800 R.E.
Vitamin D (micrograms of cholecalciferol)[2]	5 μg.	5 μg.
Vitamin E (milligrams of alpha-tocopherol equivalents)[3]	10 mg.	8 mg.
WATER-SOLUBLE VITAMINS		
Vitamin C	60 mg.	60 mg.
Thiamin (vitamin B_1)	1.2 mg.	1.0 mg.
Riboflavin (vitamin B_2)	1.4 mg.	1.2 mg.
Niacin (milligrams of niacin equivalents)[4]	16 mg.	13 mg.
Folacin	0.4 mg.	0.4 mg.
Vitamin B_6	2.2 mg.	2.0 mg.
Vitamin B_{12}	3.0 μg.	3.0 μg.
MINERALS		
Calcium	800 mg.	800 mg.
Phosphorus	800 mg.	800 mg.
Iodine	150 μg.	150 μg.
Iron	10 mg.	10 mg.
Magnesium	350 mg.	300 mg.
Zinc	15 mg.	15 mg.

[1] 1 retinol equivalent = 1 μg. retinol or 6 μg. β-carotene.
[2] 5 μg. cholecalciferol = 200 I.U. vitamin D.
[3] 1 mg. d-α-tocopherol = 1 α-tocopherol equivalent.
[4] 1 niacin equivalent = 1 mg. of niacin or 60 mg. of dietary tryptophan.
Adapted from *Recommended Dietary Allowances,* Ninth Edition (1980), with the permission of the National Academy of Sciences, Washington, D.C.

A discussion of some specific nutrients follows:

Calcium. Calcium is needed to maintain normal bone density. Adults who have symptoms of osteoporosis should receive at least 1,000 mg. daily. Calcium loss may be the cause of many lower back pain complaints, and is greater in patients confined to beds or wheelchairs. One cup of whole milk contains 285 mg. of calcium; one cup of skimmed milk has 300 mg.

Iron. Iron is required for the synthesis of hemoglobin and myoglobin and is needed in the diet at all ages. The best food sources of iron are fish and meat (fish is preferred). The iron in eggs, spinach, and some other vegetables forms insoluble salts with phosphates and phytates, thus making much of it unavailable for absorption.

Advertising claims have convinced many elderly persons that over-the-counter iron preparations will give them real pep. But in a normal person with adequate iron stores, only 10 per cent of the iron in iron-containing preparations or foods will actually be absorbed.

Caution must be observed in using iron supplements. There is a limit to the amount of iron the body can store, and excessive amounts can lead to iron storage disease and liver damage. This is not uncommon in the elderly who take iron supplements without proper guidance and care.

Zinc. Zinc is necessary for growth and is a vital component of many essential body enzymes. It seems to accelerate wound healing and may be beneficial for treating pressure sores in older, bedridden patients. Dietary fiber increases the need for zinc by decreasing its availability.

Potassium. Potassium deficiency is not unusual among older persons. An elderly man or woman needs about 60 mEq. per day, and an insufficient intake may cause muscle weakness, apathy or depression, cramps, fecal impaction, constipation, paralytic ileus, and decreased cardiac output. In severe, prolonged potassium depletion, the cells in the kidneys, heart, and skeletal muscles may be irreversibly damaged.

Sufficient amounts of potassium can be obtained solely from dietary sources. Potassium-rich foods include oranges, bananas, apricots, and many other fruits and vegetables.

Potassium supplements are rarely required and should be

used with caution. Large doses can cause potassium intoxication, with symptoms such as sharp or persistent abdominal discomfort, stiffening of the fingers, and metallic taste. If symptoms occur, potassium supplementation should be discontinued immediately.

Protein. Healthy elderly men need at least 56 gm. of protein daily; healthy elderly women, 46 gm. Protein requirements are greater in the elderly, because hypochlorhydria frequently diminishes the ability to absorb nutrients. Since the elderly often have limited nutritional reserves, the effects of stress caused by fever, malabsorption, indigestion, or poor metabolism can create a greater demand for protein.

Carbohydrates. Carbohydrates should provide at least 58 per cent of the total energy from the diet. As a rule, carbohydrate intake should decrease with increasing age; however, too great a decrease can cause any of the following problems:

- Loss of tissue protein.
- Rise in blood cholesterol due to mobilization of fat.
- Lack of energy due to electrolyte imbalance caused by increased sodium and water excretion.
- Constipation and other disturbances due to inadequate intake of bulk and fiber.

Intake of simple carbohydrates such as sugar should be limited. Intake of complex carbohydrates such as bread and cereals should be increased. For example, an appropriate goal in some cases might be to double the daily intake of bread and cereals, with a corresponding decrease in dietary fats and refined sugar. Carbohydrate intake should be spaced evenly throughout the day to stimulate insulin secretion.

Fats. Fat intake can vary greatly depending on local or family dietary habits. For example, elderly persons living on or near farms who regularly raise or purchase beef can consume as much as 10 times more fat than suburban or city dwellers. Other farm foods such as cracklings and pickled pigs' feet, the use of lard for seasoning, and frequent servings of pork can increase the fat content of the blood to dangerous levels. Special cravings may develop for foods seasoned or cooked with fats, since flavor is enhanced. Consciously or unconsciously, many disadvantaged and chronically poor elderly people prefer fatty foods because they "fill the belly" and satisfy hunger pains. Nevertheless, it is important to reduce fat intake to a minimum. With a low-fat diet, supplements of the fat-soluble vitamins A, D, and E should be taken.

Vitamins. The elderly are a high-risk group when it comes to vitamin deficiency. Contributing factors include inadequate vitamin intake, absorption disturbances, and increased vitamin requirements brought on by stress or serious illness.

Usual doses of water-soluble vitamins such as B-complex and C may be taken by the elderly without fear of toxic reaction. Excessive intake of vitamin C may cause diarrhea or watery stools and an increased potential for kidney stones.

A lifetime of poor eating habits and neglect can't be fully counterbalanced by a few weeks or months of proper nutrition in an institution. But major improvement is possible through nutritional and vitamin therapy. It's never too late to start helping a patient.

7

THE INSTITUTIONALIZED ELDERLY

Although only about 4 to 5 per cent of the aged are institutionalized, they contribute disproportionately to certain stereotypes. Four or five is a small percentage, but it still involves a large number of lives. The families of these people are deeply affected as well. How to handle Mom's or Dad's living in a nursing home is inevitably a tough emotional problem for many families.

INSTITUTIONALIZATION SYNDROME

A great deal has been said about institutionalization and its syndrome (e.g., Donaldson, 1976). Institutionalization may be defined as the isolation of a group of people in a confined location to control their activities and separate them from society at large. Institutionalization syndrome has been identified in a number of settings. Adaptation to the institutional setting, with its confinement and regimentation, also destroys independence and initiative. The resident becomes helpless and unable to make and carry out plans. Perhaps criminal behavior or mental illness may justify this result, but aging is neither a crime nor a sickness.

An incisive study of a Massachusetts nursing home documented this phenomenon in the institutionalized elderly. The residents who learned to "play the game" and live by the institution's rules thrived; those who didn't adapt didn't survive.

Earlier observations on children in orphanages and experiments on monkeys deprived of their mothers revealed a similar passivity and helplessness. The children lagged far behind normal youngsters in their development. The monkeys failed to interact normally with other monkeys. Also, many an experimental psychologist has found that laboratory rats who learned complicated mazes well failed to adapt to the outside world after being released.

Sharon Curtin (1972) has suggested how the custodial attitude in institutions for the elderly—the staff members' belief that old people are incapable of benefiting from treatment—contributes to institutionalization syndrome. One poignant incident she described was an attempted exchange between two old people who had been transported to the solarium of a nursing home; as they acknowledged each other and started a conversation the nurses separated them as though this display of energy might be too much effort and shock the other residents.

Curtin describes a number of other situations in which old people were treated like children—in some cases, bizarrely so. For example, the elderly residents in one home were persuaded to don masks and "make merry as children" for a Halloween party. Curtin also suggests the reason for the custodial attitude so often seen in nursing homes. In many instances the old people are there to live out the rest of their lives. Although statistically this will be often a number of years, neither the residents nor the staff want to accept that fact. It's as though staff members aren't clear in their own minds as to whether the nursing home is primarily a residence or a hospital. Being medically trained, they tend to resolve the conflict on the side of the hospital, with its orientation geared toward efficiency and restrictions. The fact that some nursing-home residents are genuinely sick may add to this tendency.

Many nursing-home administrators have complained that standard nursing training is inappropriate for workers in a nursing home. They point out the need for special training more appropriate to the needs of nursing-home residents, although definite resistance and misinterpretation of programs that explore the values of the nursing-home system have been encountered (see Chapters 11 and 12 and Appendices 1, 2, and 3).

WHO ARE THE INSTITUTIONALIZED ELDERLY?

About half the institutionalized elderly are diagnosed as having chronic brain syndrome (C.B.S.), also called organic brain syndrome (O.B.S.). C.B.S. has four symptoms: (1) a sudden, noticeable loss of memory; (2) loss of orientation to time, places, persons, or events; (3) mental disorganization, shown by so-called word salads; and (4) emotional lability—sudden, drastic changes in mood (Linden, 1974). Jarvik (1976) has noted the syndrome's ambiguous nature and the strong judgmental component in its diagnosis. For instance, a depressed, mildly disorganized person with a sensory loss due to a condition like cataracts might appear to be suffering from C.B.S. In spite of this, however, the term chronic brain syndrome has been used casually and categorically as though it were the clearest of conditions to diagnose.

It's generally accepted that C.B.S. has at least two causes. One is arteriosclerosis or hardening of the arteries. It's presently thought that rigidity of the smaller blood vessels in the brain is directly responsible for C.B.S. Transport of oxygen to the brain is diminished, and the symptoms follow. Much of the research on the effects of oxygen deficit or hypoxia, such as that described by Van Lier and Stychnie (1963), supports this idea. McFarland's (1963) theory of aging is also based on data obtained under hypobaric (low oxygen) conditions. These data are consistent with the oxygen-deficit explanation.

The other principal cause of C.B.S. is deterioration of the brain, or senility. Neural structure, nutrients, and oxygen are necessary for proper brain functioning. Apparently a critical mass is necessary (Linden, 1974) for normal function. When more than that amount is destroyed, C.B.S. or senility occurs (Linden, 1974). Cross sections of brains obtained at autopsy from people who were diagnosed as having C.B.S. indicate that their brain cells had lost their weblike structure and appeared like haystacks lined up together. The interconnections among neurons had been lost. That a critical mass may be necessary for acceptable cognitive functioning is consistent with the classic results reported by the physiological psychologist Lashley (1929). Using rats, he found it was the mass of the cerebrum rather than specific locations in it that affected the performance of typical

49

learning and problem-solving tasks. Deficits in performance were generally proportional to the amount of cortex destroyed. When a critical mass was reached, the animals could no longer learn or solve problems.

DEINSTITUTIONALIZATION

Because of the problems created by institutionalization, today there's a movement away from it. The recognition that mental hospitals and nursing homes can cause more problems than they solve has strongly motivated this movement (Linden, 1974). The finding on psychiatric casualties of World War II, that many tended to live up to their "craziness" labels when in fact they weren't hopelessly insane, undoubtedly has also contributed to the deinstitutionalization philosophy.

Many who have worked in institutions have argued that a large percentage of the patients who are allowed or "persuaded" to leave refuse to do so; if they do leave, they waste away outside the institution and return before too much time has passed. These incidents, the same workers suggest, prove that disturbed people are rightfully kept confined. These arguments tend to ignore the fact that many of these patients are simply displaying the effects of the institutionalization itself—dependency and an inability to adapt to a self-regulated environment (Fleishman and McKenna, 1975).

In some cases these criticisms are rationalizations by incompetent workers who are afraid of losing their jobs. The majority of nursing-home and hospital workers, however, are conscientious professionals who resent being thought of as wardens, custodians, or jailers. They feel, with some justification, that everyone in the system is treated as human but themselves. Well-conducted training programs for workers in institutional settings emphasize the importance of their feelings. Trainers need to set good examples in their own conduct and encourage staff members to communicate with each other; staff members, in turn, should encourage residents to do the same. These are the objectives of many staff training programs and remotivation therapy, a form of group therapy for nursing-home residents and mental patients (see Chapter 12).

The advent of mood-altering drugs, such as tranquilizers and antidepressants, in the early 1950s has helped make deinstitutionalization possible. These drugs, though perhaps overprescribed (Whittaker and Fleishman, 1976), have virtually emptied the back wards of state mental hospitals and made straitjackets and padded cells practically obsolete. That elderly and mildly disturbed people are better off in a free environment than in a custodial setting is now generally accepted. This trend has led to widespread outpatient care and routine medication. The use of medications for old people, however, ought to be regarded as temporary; the goal of treatment should be a return to free, independent living, if at all possible.

The Federal Government encourages outpatient care in the community for the elderly and mildly disturbed, through grants made by the National Institute of Mental Health to support paraprofessional staff for locally administered outpatient programs (Linden, 1974).

In 1975 the Supreme Court provided legal backing for deinstitutionalization. It declared that residents of institutions who are dangerous neither to themselves nor to others, who are capable of financially supporting themselves, and who are not receiving treatment have the right to be released. Donaldson (1976) has written about his personal experiences within the mental institutional system, and of course *One Flew Over the Cuckoo's Nest* has brought many injustices to the public attention. Many patients have been released and are being released from institutions only because of their legal rights; that there are so many of these people is a most cogent argument that mental hospitals have sometimes acted as prisons.

Many of the staff in these hospitals have admitted informally (Fleishman and McKenna, 1975) that deinstitutionalization has great merit but that it's too late for patients who have spent years in a hospital. They also state that paying patients to stay in the hospital (e.g., with veterans' benefits) sabotages the movement. Finally, they feel that not enough has been done to prepare the patient and the community for release. This point has also been made by Adlestein (1976). Without family and/or community acceptance of the patient and understanding of mental illness, this movement may be seriously weakened. With community orientation, however, outpatient care and halfway houses may become the usual settings for treatment of mild mental disorders.

COMMUNITY OUTPATIENT CLINICS

Psychiatrists have taken a strong stand in favor of holistic care of the aged patient. (Holistic approaches, such as Goldstein's [1943], emphasize treatment of the entire person.) Duke University, with the help of its psychiatry department and particularly Dr. Eric Pfeiffer, has set up a strong geriatrics and gerontology program. Dr. Maurice Linden, a classically trained psychoanalyst, has been a pioneer in this field and a strong advocate for the elderly. Dr. Joseph Adlestein, a psychiatrist and pioneer in the public health field, has helped start a holistically oriented medical program for the aged at Harrisburg (Pennsylvania) Hospital that considers both medical and social problems. In the 1960s Dr. Frank F. Furstenberg, an internist, helped set up a program oriented toward older persons' medical and social needs at Sinai Hospital in Baltimore; it has become a very effective geriatric program. Drs. Robert Butler and Elisabeth Kübler-Ross, both psychiatrists, are well known for their insights into aging.

Dr. Linden heads a medical program that is an outstanding example of an alternative to institutionalization of the elderly. His eight-point program, outlined below, works very effectively in a conservative South Philadelphia community. Its values are consistent with the community's, Dr. Linden's innovative work in psychiatry, and the movement toward deinstitutionalization.

The Jefferson Community Center, as it's called, offers eight services: treatment of (1) chronic brain syndrome, (2) acute brain syndrome, (3) malnutrition, (4) depression, and (5) psychosis, as well as (6) education of the family and community, (7) general medical and surgical care, and (8) prevention and treatment of social breakdown.

Dr. Linden subscribes to the egalitarian value system in mental hospitals. This value system became the basis for programs funded by the National Institute of Mental Health. The egalitarian philosophy holds that (1) effective treatment requires a group contribution; (2) psychiatric treatment is an interpersonal process, not only electroshock, drugs, and so forth, which are threatening and impersonal; (3) all people possess insight and are potential therapists; (4) the patient's positive aspects, not the debilitating ones, should be emphasized; (5) the patient is an active participant in his treatment; and (6) the institutional boundaries are penetrable and the program is part of the community. The ideal is to create a supportive and therapeutic community whose entire staff is involved in treatment of patients, under the direction of physicians.

The symptoms of C.B.S. were discussed earlier in this chapter. Acute brain syndrome (A.B.S.) has the same symptoms as C.B.S., but they are transient and disappear relatively shortly after onset. The major causes of A.B.S. are cerebrovascular accidents, malnutrition, and incorrect or excessive medication.

Frequently an older person suffering an aneurysm or a temporary slowdown in the circulation of blood to the brain will display A.B.S. After adequate circulation has been restored, the symptoms disappear. Many stroke victims suffer a temporary, severe decrease in circulation to portions of the brain. They recover fairly quickly if there has not been severe loss of brain tissue and if blood supply is available through collateral vessels; this is true at any age.

Malnutrition, a general problem in itself for the aged, is a common reason for A.B.S. Frequently older people forget to eat because of the lack of company and social structure in their lives. Combined with these problems may be the relative dullness of their hunger pangs as a result of general sensory losses, the difficulty of shopping for one person, trouble getting to the store, and lack of money for food. The resulting malnutrition will sometimes produce confusion and disorientation.

Drug interactions are a severe problem for the elderly. Old people who "shop" from one doctor to another may get prescriptions for several different drugs to handle their emotional and physical complaints. Sometimes they take these drugs incorrectly; the drugs can accumulate or interact, causing A.B.S. Hospitalization may be necessary.

Linden (1974) cited a study by Goldsmith that reported a 4 to 18 per cent spontaneous recovery rate among the elderly admitted to state hospitals and attributed it to the eating of decent food for a reasonable period of time. That dietary deficiencies often lead to dramatic illnesses is well known. Pellagra is due to niacin (a B-complex vitamin) deficiency. This deficiency leads to diarrhea, dermatitis, dementia, and death. The psychological symptoms are dramatic, but they disappear with proper vitamin therapy. Beriberi, a disease due to thiamin (also a B-complex vitamin) deficiency, produces a state of severe anxiety that quickly disappears with proper diet. In addition to these drastic conditions, malnutrition and lack of a balanced diet may cause general listlessness and lethargy and probably are important contributors to the slowness, confusion, or malaise observed in some aged people. Linden (1974) often prescribes vitamin injections for the old as an integral part of their treatment in order to restore missing vitamins B and C. These injections also seem to increase absorption in the intestinal walls, improving nutrition.

Depression is one of the most common emotional problems experienced by the aged (Blum, 1976; Busse and Pfeiffer, 1969). With the grim losses they face this isn't surprising; however, depression can also be caused by physical disorders as well as social isolation and intrinsic psychological factors (Linden, 1974). If not treated early, depression tends to worsen, and according to some authorities it may be the start of mental illness in general. As a mildly depressed person grows older, he loses many of his psychological props, so it becomes especially necessary to give his emotional state prompt attention (Linden, 1974).

Psychosis is also treated at the Jefferson Community Center. Often it's an escape from unbearable realities the patient faces. It needs to be treated promptly because it tends to cause the patient to regress. The patient's family situation may often have contributed to his psychosis.

Parent-child conflicts may often be put on the back burner when the child marries and leaves home. When Mom or Dad comes to live with a married child, however, the same antagonisms, hostility, and bitterness start to boil up again. Dr. Virginia Hall (1976) has suggested, perhaps not entirely facetiously, forming a society for the prevention of cruelty to old parents. Unhealthy parent-child interactions require that the entire family receive therapy and counseling on how to cope with each other. Often, to escape chronic conflicts, the child places the parent in an institution. This creates heavy guilt feelings for the child and institutionalization problems for the older person. Nursing-home personnel encounter these familial problems all the time and need to offer programs that prepare and counsel the family on how to handle their feelings. Such programs could also make it easier for the staff to handle patients.

Another important role of the Jefferson Community Center is educating the community and the families of its elderly clients about their own and others' aging. Guided discussions on the meaning of old age, what to expect, how to prepare for it, and how to get help are part of the program. The importance of community involvement and public understanding and acceptance of aging are essential to effective, lasting programs for the aged. Only when "you" and "I" become "we," and we are able to see ourselves as sharing the same experiences, can a dent be made in the wall of misconceptions surrounding the experience of aging. It's interesting to consider what would happen if we could see that when we concern ourselves with remedying human afflictions, we're actually talking about how we ourselves want to be treated.

Common medical and surgical disorders make up the seventh class of problems treated. Older people sometimes use physical discomforts as a pretext for going to the doctor when actually they need help with emotional problems. Many of them tend to view emotional problems as a sign of weakness, and their pride and defenses make it difficult to acknowledge psychological problems directly. The medical services not only are essential to health care but also open the door for elderly patients to air their less tangible problems.

During the past several years there has been an increase in surgery for the elderly. The medical profession's attitude toward corrective surgery for the aged has changed; operations that weren't done several years ago—e.g., for gallbladder, arthritic, heart, or circulatory ailments—are now performed safely and routinely on elderly patients.

Social breakdown syndrome, a typical form of alienation of the elderly from the surrounding community, is important to acknowledge and understand. The elderly may rank their various losses according to their degree of severity (Linden, 1974): They range from loss of status, to loss of personal worth, to loss of independence, to loss of mental capacity, to accepting institution-alization, and, finally, to loss of life itself. Each is a stage of deterioration of personal identity. Whereas traditional cultures—Mexico's, for example—revere their aged and see these people as positive contributors to society, thus reinforcing their sense of personal identity, our culture's nontraditional attitudes tend to make them feel unwanted and unneeded. Viewing someone positively, giving him love, and helping him take his inevitable losses in stride (Taylor, 1974) and as settling forces (Pollak, 1973, 1976) can help an aged person keep his personal identity and dignity. These issues are also of primary concern at the Jefferson Community Center.

Encouraging social cooperation has been a consistent part of Linden's professional value system. His eight-point program is directed toward the whole person and, in many respects, toward the whole community. By helping and sharing with each other, its members also help themselves.

References

Adlestein, J. Personal communication, 1976.

Blum, J. Paper presented at Continuing Education Conference on Psychodynamics of Aging at New York University Postgraduate Center for Mental Health, New York, 1976.

Busse, E., and Pfeiffer, E., eds. *Behavior and Adaptation in Late Life.* Little, Brown, Boston, 1969.

Curtin, S. *Nobody Ever Died of Old Age.* Little, Brown, Boston, 1972.

Donaldson, G. *Insanity Inside Out.* Crown, New York, 1976.

Fleishman, J., and McKenna, C. Unpublished study, 1975.

Goldstein, K. "Concerning Rigidity." *Character and Personality* 11:209–226, 1943.

Hall, V. Personal communication, 1976.

Jarvik, L. Paper presented at Continuing Education Conference on Psychodynamics of Aging at New York University Postgraduate Center for Mental Health, New York, 1976.

Lashley, K.S. *Brain Mechanisms and Intelligence.* University of Chicago Press, Chicago, 1929.

Linden, M. Paper presented at Continuing Education Conference on Society and the Aging at Harrisburg Area Community College, Harrisburg, Pa., 1974.

McFarland, R. In *Hypoxia* (Van Lier, E., and Stychnie, J., eds.). University of Chicago Press, Chicago, 1963.

Pollak, O. Paper presented at Continuing Education Conference on Psychodynamics of Aging at New York University Postgraduate Center for Mental Health, New York, 1976.

Pollak, O. Paper presented at S.I.E.C.U.S. Conference, Philadelphia, 1973.

Rich, T., and Gilmore, A. *Basic Concepts of Aging—A Programmed Manual.* U.S. Government Printing Office, Washington, D.C., 1972.

Taylor, C. Paper presented at Continuing Education Conference on Society and the Aging at Harrisburg Area Community College, Harrisburg, Pa., 1974.

Van Lier, E., and Stychnie, J., eds. *Hypoxia.* University of Chicago Press, Chicago, 1963.

Whittaker, J., and Fleishman, J. "Biological Foundations of Psychology: Behavior and States of Awareness." In *Introduction to Psychology,* 3rd ed. Saunders, Philadelphia, 1976.

SEXUALITY

Sex, one of our strongest drives, isn't discussed openly at any age. Privately we seek insight into the role sex plays in our lives, and any reasonably good book on the subject is bound to make the best-seller lists. Our general ignorance of sexuality is especially acute when it comes to telling the elderly how to behave sexually. In effect, we deny their desire and ability to keep on practicing what they've enjoyed most of their adult lives.

Why do we expect people to lose their sexual drive as they grow older? The "dirty old man" image implies that lust, desire, and the willingness to share love are perversions in the elderly. The many jokes about older people and sex may also reflect fears about our own sexual performance; perhaps they're a way of rationalizing a lackluster episode as due to "getting old."

These expectations imply that we still view sex as an obligation. Maybe older people, whose reproductive years are over, are seen as glad to give it up. Or perhaps we feel that because aging often brings impaired health it also impairs sexuality.

WHAT IS SEXUALITY?

Sexuality is a special kind of communication between people that involves physical contact and pleasurable psychological arousal. It's a direct way of expressing strong affection and love. A frequent misconception about sexuality is that it's the same as coitus. Any definition that views coitus as necessary to human sexuality overemphasizes the physical sex act. Coitus can, of course, result in conception, and a man and woman may want to express their love for each other by having a baby. But any definition that views conception as the purpose of sex is narrow and

59

moralistic. Touching, expressing love, physical and psychological arousal, and coitus are all parts of sexuality. We don't expect
an elderly couple to stop loving each other; there's no reason to
expect them to stop expressing that love sexually.

SEXUAL NORMS FOR THE AGED

Pfeiffer (1973) reported an extensive study that explored the
sexual attitudes and activities of the aged. Interestingly, the people interviewed liked talking about their sexuality. However, the
young professionals who interviewed them reported they felt
uncomfortable asking older people questions about sex. The
adult children of the aged were very concerned that the study
intruded into their parents' privacy and also expressed personal
embarrassment.

Two hundred fifty people, including 31 married couples,
were interviewed. In checking the reliability of their answers it
was found that spouses independently agreed with each other 90
per cent of the time.

The results showed that sex plays an important role in the
lives of people in their 60s, 70s, 80s, and 90s. Of men in their late
60s it was found that:

- 80 per cent were interested in sex;
- 50 per cent participated regularly (on the average of once a
  week or more).

Ten years later, in the same group:

- 25 per cent were still sexually active on a regular basis;
- Some decreased the frequency of their sexual activity, some
  stayed the same, and a few increased their frequency.

For women in their late 60s it was found that:

- 50 per cent had continued interest in sex;
- 30 per cent were sexually active on a regular basis.

Ten years later, of the same women:

- 30 per cent had continued sexual interest;
- 20 per cent still enjoyed sex regularly.

When the men were asked why they stopped having sex they
blamed themselves. When the married women were asked why
they stopped, "It was him" was the frequent answer. Thus generally it was the man who ceased sex in a marriage. For unmar-
ried women stopping was blamed on lack of a partner.

There were other interesting findings:
- Sexual experience early in life is related to sexual activity in old age; those who had strong interest in sex during their early years remained interested;
- It's not true that "you can wear it out";
- Physical health is related to sexuality in old age;
- For men, marital status made no difference in sexual activity;
- Only married women reported an active sex life.

Women outlive men by an average of eight years, and thus are subject to approximately 12 years of widowhood (men are four years older than their spouses on the average). Maggie Kuhn (1973), head of the Gray Panthers, has offered a cogent argument for marriage between older women and younger men, based on these statistics. Widowers have an ample field to play while widows do not. The frequent cry from older women, "A good man is hard to find," is thus a realistic complaint.

PHYSICAL ASPECTS

The same study (Pfeiffer, 1973) also showed that where impotence existed, very little of it was due to organic causes. Sexuality still remained strongly a matter of state of mind. Because it's more difficult to become aroused as sensory sensitivity decreases with advancing age, touching assumes more importance as a sexual expression. Once sexual arousal occurs, however, it tends to last longer. Sexual pleasure is the same for the elderly as for the younger generation.

HOW SOCIAL ATTITUDES CAN HELP

We often treat the elderly very foolishly as far as sexuality is concerned. We tend to be insensitive to their needs and discourage remarriage when remarriage may be an excellent idea. Sexual relations between old people seem to embarrass their children and spark conflicts and disbelief about their physical relationship that go back to adolescence. "Other people's parents make love—but *mine?*" This sentiment seems to linger far beyond childhood.

Because our society doesn't acknowledge that sex can be an important part of later life, old people with sex problems tend to encounter indifference, disbelief, or scorn when they ask for help (Lief, 1973). Doctors are sometimes the worst offenders. One pragmatic and understanding housing manager of an apartment complex for the aged is said to encourage the tenants to keep up their love lives by approving their expressions of mutual interest and, when possible, even arranging for adjacent apartments when a liaison seems likely to last. This natural, casual attitude keeps morale high.

References

Kuhn, M. Paper presented at S.I.E.C.U.S. Conference, Philadelphia, 1973.

Lief, A. Paper presented at S.I.E.C.U.S. Conference, Philadelphia, 1973.

Pfeiffer, E. Paper presented at S.I.E.C.U.S. Conference, Philadelphia, 1973.

9

DEALING WITH DEATH

SOCIAL ATTITUDES TOWARD DEATH

Our society makes strenuous efforts to protect its young from contact with death. As we enter our middle years we seem to awaken to the possibility of our own death (Pollak, 1973). We're more likely to know someone facing death and even more likely to know someone who's mourning a dead relative. Our early protection from death, while well intended, leaves us exceptionally vulnerable to emotional shock when we do encounter it. We have to learn all at once how to cope with the anticipated loss of our own life or that of a loved one. We suddenly become aware that the reality of death is very remote from the idealized and perhaps religious or euphemistic conceptions of it that we were taught as children. The price that has to be paid for this ignorance is emotionally draining, but dealing with death helps complete our maturity. Because our society is secretive about death, there's a lack of useful knowledge on the subject.

DEATH AS A PART OF LIFE

There's one fate all human beings have in common—death, dying, losing oneself, and the awareness of it. Arthur Koestler has spoken of the uniqueness and delicate nature of that awareness. The ability to anticipate our own death and reflect on it distinguishes us from all other species. We may wonder whether there will be a world without us; Linden (1976) has pointed out the egocentricity intrinsic to our thoughts on our own death.

Death provides the background against which all life occurs. The greatest risk of living is the ultimate mistake—to cause one's own death. Most theories regarding death focus on our vulnerability to the thought of it and how our perception of death helps shape personality. Although open discussion of dying has been rare in this society, there's convincing evidence of our omnipresent concern with it. It's hard to think of a religion without a view on death.

For the aged death becomes a very close, real consideration. As friends and relatives of the same generation die, the elderly tend to take a pragmatic interest in funerals, cemeteries, wills, and estates. This interest isn't morbid but reflects an acknowledgment that death is inevitable.

DYING WITH DIGNITY

Dying with dignity is of greater concern to the elderly than the simple realization that death is inevitable. The awareness that one may lose control of bodily functions is especially frightening. For example, an 87-year-old woman living in a nursing home had hardening of the arteries and chronic brain syndrome. Frequently she acted paranoid, accusing people of harming her. Part of her paranoia probably came from loss of sight and hearing. She had lost sphincter control and had to rely on others to move her. She had special religious dietary needs the nursing home couldn't meet. There was no hope of cure. She had already cut her social ties and could never return to her home. This woman told her daughter how miserable and undignified she felt: "That life has come to this! I'd rather be dead."

Heifetz and Mangel (1976) have written extensively about the patient's right to die with dignity. They even suggest it's the physician's responsibility to prevent the indignities of biological vegetation and the emotional and financial drain it imposes on the family. The ethics they espouse warrants serious thought. They share with the reader the human emotional component of dying as well as the biological aspects. They also describe hospices—places where dying people receive sympathetic care but no attempt is made to prolong their lives (see end of chapter).

HOW THE ELDERLY APPROACH DEATH

Elisabeth Kübler-Ross has achieved great acclaim for her studies on how people face death, one aspect of the field of thanatology. Her work contains profound insights. What occurs when people face death is actually quite different from what we might expect. Perhaps more than anything else, dying people don't want to be left alone or made to feel useless in this last confrontation of their lives. Kübler-Ross (1975) sums up: "This is perhaps the greatest lesson we learned from our patients: LIVE, so you do not have to look back and say: 'God, how I have wasted my life.' "

The one point she emphasizes over all others, however, is that it's never too late while alive to share feelings, communicate with others, and overcome isolation and loneliness—the essentials of human growth. She illustrates this idea in the following touching passage (1975) that describes the reactions of dying patients to being asked to share their innermost feelings in a seminar on dying:

> The patients who were asked to serve were no problem either. They were often quite grateful to be "useful," to feel that someone needed them rather than the other way around. When we started to talk they quickly overcame their initial shyness and rather quickly shared with us the fantastic loneliness they felt. Strangers whom we had never met shared their grief, their isolation, their inability to talk about their illness and death with their next-of-kin. They expressed their anger at the physician who did not "level" with them, at the minister who tried to console them with the too often repeated phrase "It is God's will," or at friends and relatives who visited them with the inevitable "Cheer up, it's not so bad." We learned to identify quickly with them and became much more sensitive to their needs and fears than ever before. They taught us a great deal about living and dying, and they appreciated our asking them to be our teachers.

In a particularly poignant anecdote, Kübler-Ross (1975) describes the effects of the teaching seminar on a social worker at the hospital who had been working with the family of a dying patient. The social worker reflected on the changes she experienced as a result of discussing death:

> I had a similar problem in working with many aged and infirm clients in the past years. I always felt that old age and sickness was so devastating, that although I

wanted to communicate hope to them, I only communicated despair. I think that the seminar has helped me to see that life did not have to end in mental and physical agony.

In reflecting upon what was learned in counseling the dying patients, the same worker continued: "In working with any patient, there must be a goal toward which you both are striving and some belief that movement to resolution or comfort is possible. It seems to me from observations of the interviews that listening itself is a comfort to these patients." In recalling a dying man who was unable to convey to his wife the loneliness and other feelings he was experiencing, the social worker added:

I think another great help a social worker can give is to the family of the dying patient—not so much in the way stressed by so much of the casework literature (homemaker, financial aid, etc.) but in helping them to relate better to the patient. Mr. N. wanted to talk about his illness to his wife and she to him. But they were each afraid to cause the other pain and did not know how much the other knew. With reassurance from the staff, Mrs. N. was able to broach the subject with her husband and they were then able to share and to be a source of comfort to each other—instead of suffering alone.

More recently Kübler-Ross (1976) has noted that her work with dying people has led to some interesting cross-cultural findings concerning the memories of patients who were revived after being diagnosed as clinically dead. This has stirred up quite a controversy.

DEATH IN AN INSTITUTIONAL SETTING

Since many dying people are in hospitals or nursing homes, it becomes the doctor's job to handle their approach to death. In many respects this is the poorest choice (Kübler-Ross, 1975). Doctors have as much trouble as anyone in coping with death, perhaps more so because of their commitment to fighting it. Because they regard death as a personal defeat, many doctors may be unable to share with patients the emotions involved in openly facing death.

Being in an institution can compound the dying patient's

problems. The institution is restrictive and regimented; it's emotionally sterile and lacks the vitality found in places where healthy people are free to make decisions and mistakes. It's no wonder so many terminal patients want to go home to die. Along with others, Dr. Kübler-Ross has made it evident that we need to talk more openly about death with dying patients and to stop overprotecting them from knowledge of their condition.

HOSPICES

For terminally ill patients who prefer an alternative to traditional care in a hospital, there is a rapidly growing concept sweeping the nation—hospice. Hospice is an old word with a new meaning. The old word refers to a medieval way station where a weary pilgrim could stop for refreshments during a long journey. The new birth of the word implies "living until we die." This is encouraged by using highly specialized health-care techniques emphasizing the management of pain and other symptoms associated with terminal illness. The hospice concept provides care and concern for the patient, family, and close friends. The hospice-care team includes physicians, nurses, social workers, clergymen, allied health-care providers, and trained volunteers.

The hospice concept can be implemented in a hospital setting, nursing or convalescent center, hospice facility, or in the comfort of the patient's own home or apartment—which appears to be the most feasible and satisfying situation for most dying patients.

The hospice movement is gaining popularity throughout the United States. Hospice provides a humanistic manner of dealing with terminally ill patients and their families and friends. It also provides an alternative to the enormous costs usually associated with short- or long-term care of dying patients in traditional health-care environments.

In implementing the hospice concept there are three main goals:

- To ease the physical discomfort of the terminally ill patient by employing pharmaceutical and advanced clinical techniques for effective symptom control.
- To ease the psychological discomfort of the terminally ill patient through programs allowing for active participation in

scheduled activities or periods of peaceful withdrawal as determined by the patient.

• To aid in maintaining the emotional equilibrium of the patient and the family as they go through the traumatic life experience of progressive disease and ultimately the final separation of death.

Volunteer training is an integral part of the hospice program. The volunteer, selected from the community, becomes a part of the health-care team and identifies with an individual patient. The volunteer works with the patient and family giving support, running errands, easing burdens, and remains during the period of bereavement.

The hospice concept views death as a natural process of life. It is a humane and peaceful method of treatment for the dying and their families.

The *Locator Directory of Hospices in America,* published by the National Hospice Organization (NHO), lists all recognized hospice programs in the United States. For information, contact:

National Hospice Organization
1311A Dolly Madison Boulevard
McLean, Va. 22101
(703) 356-6770

References

Heifetz, M.D., and Mangel, C. *The Right to Die.* Berkley Publishing Corp., New York, 1976.

Kohut, J. J. Unpublished observations, 1981.

Kübler-Ross, E. *Death: The Final Stage of Growth.* Spectrum Books, New York, 1975.

Kübler-Ross, E. "In Her Own Words." *People* magazine, pp. 66–69, November 24, 1976.

Linden, M. Personal communication, 1976.

Maikel, W.M., and Sinon, V. *The Hospice Concept.* American Cancer Society, Inc., New York, 1978.

Perrallay, L., and Mallica, M. "Public Knowledge of Hospice Care." *Nursing Outlook,* pp. 46–48, January, 1981.

Pollak, O. Paper presented at S.I.E.C.U.S. Conference, Philadelphia, 1973.

10

BRIDGING THE GAP BETWEEN THEORY AND PRACTICE

The preceding chapters have described the challenges confronting the elderly and what happens during the aging process. The sociology and psychological aspects of aging and the physical changes and special needs of old people have been spelled out.

Gerontologists and geriatric medical and social-service workers are helping awaken the public conscience to the problems of aging and are introducing new ideas, refreshing attitudes, and even new terminology. Applying research findings and new training techniques to improve life for the aged should be a national priority. The establishment of the National Institute on Aging (N.I.A.) is a monumental step toward enhancing the quantity and quality of life for the elderly through the funding of scientific investigations. While it's important to understand and disseminate theoretical and interdisciplinary discoveries that can result in better care for the elderly, it's necessary first to shatter the many myths and stereotypes associated with the aged and the process of growing old. With the rapidly developing theoretical interest in the elderly, there must be a corresponding practical application of new techniques that benefit both the institutionalized and the home-bound elderly. A bridge must be built to connect the theoretical with the practical and clinical if the quality of everyday life for the elderly is to be significantly improved. This can be done not only in hospitals and nursing homes but also in the many innovative programs—home health care, day care, senior citizens' centers, outreach clinics, Meals on Wheels, and congregate feeding—that have been developed to assist the elderly in many communities.

When an elderly person enters an institution, the orientation or intake process begins with a comprehensive assessment of his capabilities—physical, psychological, social, cognitive, and functional. A relocation therapy program makes the move from a familiar home to the health-care facility easier. A psychological condition called transfer trauma is likely to occur when the elderly, especially if they're confused, are moved from one place to another, even from floor to floor in the same nursing home. The end result of transfer trauma is serious illness. It's shocking but true that 65 per cent of all American elderly moving from one nursing home to another die within six months (Nursing Home Relocation Team, 1976). Therefore relocation therapy is often a prerequisite for survival.

A program of reality orientation (Chapter 11) or remotivation therapy (Chapter 12) may be warranted for the bewildered institutionalized man or woman. Many facilities provide additional social, psychological, and physical incentives like music, occupational, vocational, recreational, physical, and psychosocial therapy. Counseling patients on death and dying and pre- and post-retirement and legal-rights seminars and workshops are becoming standard and even mandatory offerings in some health-care facilities.

Therapy, modality, and practical treatment programs must be born out of an understanding derived from scientific conclusions about the aging process. Chapter 7 gives a scientific definition of chronic or organic brain syndrome. Someone who suffers from C.B.S. needs help, not pity. Reality orientation (R.O.) is a systematic program for helping badly confused people. For many of them it can restore a rich and productive life. Reorientation is the first step in the psychological rehabilitation of the confused, disoriented patient. There's a direct correlation between someone's ability to function adequately in his environment and his degree of orientation to that environment. R.O. provides a special awareness and a structured course of action for all members of the health-care team—nurses, physicians, nurse's aides, occupational and physical therapists, orderlies, food-service workers, volunteers, relatives, and friends. In today's world of educational and medical accountability, R.O. is increasingly being required by Federal, state, county, and municipal agencies and endorsed by professional accreditation associations for inclusion during preservice and in-service training of medical and nonprofessional support personnel. This educational program of improved communication includes staff training in nursing homes, hospitals, institutions for the mentally retarded, and other short- and long-term care facilities.

"We believe that the ultimate test of our research and training programs is the difference they make in the quality of life of older people," says Dr. George L. Maddox, Director of the Center for the Study of Aging and Human Development at Duke University. The following chapter, in the spirit of that statement, provides practical guidelines to the use of an R.O. program, whether it's in a private home, hospital, or other health-care facility. We're all growing older. The ultimate goal is a rich and happy life regardless of age or circumstances. This, of course, takes communication among family and friends of the patient or resident and the health-care staff.

Reference

Nursing Home Relocation Team. Commonwealth of Pennsylvania, Department of Public Welfare, Camp Hill, Pa., 1976.

11

REALITY ORIENTATION

Reality orientation is not reality therapy in a historical or even clinical sense. It is not a watered-down version of Harris's *I'm OK—You're OK*. It is not strictly a program for the elderly, but benefits both young and old. It does provide a special awareness and structured course of action for all members of the health-care team—physicians, nurses, nurse's aides, occupational and physical therapists, orderlies, food-service workers, volunteers, and the patient's relatives and friends.

Reality orientation is built on the premise that an individual's ability to function adequately in his environment is directly correlated with his degree of orientation to that environment. From facts such as date, time, place, and similar environmental clues, an individual constructs a basic framework from which his more complex patterns of behavior and daily routines develop. When someone is no longer exposed to positive, meaningful stimuli from which he can extract environmental clues, he may start to lose his ability to construct this framework. His lack of exposure, whether caused by personal limitations or social isolation, results in inappropriate, inadequate, or confused behavior. Such a person may forget where he is, who the people around him are, and what he's expected to do or say in a given situation.

Reality orientation directly addresses the problems of confused, disoriented behavior and memory loss associated with lack of social interaction and positive stimuli. In this technique, health-care personnel actively and repetitively present orientation information to an individual whenever he seems confused or disoriented. This process gives the confused person the information he needs to begin reconstructing his environmental framework. Once he starts to relocate himself in time and place, it's hoped that his inappropriate behavioral patterns will begin to change for the better and eventually disappear.

The R.O. program is also designed for the family and friends of confused persons living at home or in a long-term care facility. With an understanding of R.O. and their role in it, they can join the health-care team in assisting the confused person.

ASSESSING THE ELDERLY PATIENT

Unfortunately, many old people who appear confused are automatically labeled "senile" or "uncooperative" and the underlying cause of their behavior isn't investigated.

Confused behavior may reflect a functional disorder—that is, a disturbance of mental functioning that occurs without physiological changes in the brain. Under psychiatric care, many older patients with functional disorders have significantly restored their normal patterns of thought, speech, and activity.

On the other hand, confused behavior may result from an organic disorder associated with physiological changes that produce brain dysfunction or damage, as described in Chapter 7. Confused behavior may also result from both an organic and a functional disorder. It's almost always compounded by changes in physical environment, as when a person is hospitalized or relocated. Other contributing causes include sensory or perceptual alterations, previous behavior patterns, loss of status or independence, and the attitudes of others.

As mentioned in Chapter 7, physiological changes in the brain that produce confused or bizarre behavior may be chronic or organic, or they may be acute or of short duration. A.B.S. can be reversed by correcting the condition that caused it—malnutrition, for example. C.B.S., however, is essentially irreversible, since it results from hardening of the arteries supplying the brain and/or from deterioration of the brain tissue itself.

Although chronic brain syndromes are irreversible, under certain circumstances considerable improvement is possible in the person's relationships with others, his personal habits, and his daily activities. Thorough investigation into the cause of the confusion is needed to determine the proper handling of the confused geriatric patient.

Once the cause or causes are determined, it's the responsibility of those working or living with a confused individual to bring him back to reality. The process may be a long and tedious one, but as long as there are no signs of regression, progress is being made.

Confusion—what is it? Its symptoms can be frighteningly severe. They vary from person to person and include forgetfulness, drastic mood changes, agitation, repeated inappropriate behavior, impaired judgment and intellect, and changes in orientation to person, place, and time. Nearly every elderly patient entering a nursing home exhibits a certain amount of confusion. The separation from family and friends and the changes in environment, living habits, diet, and sleeping patterns all contribute to disorientation and depression. Separation from home and family may also cause extreme anxiety. This kind of confusion can—and should—be remedied.

Tension and anxiety further unhinge the already-confused resident. Your goal is to relax and reorient him. Most confused elderly people know they're confused—that's one reason they're so upset. They want help. If you deny their condition, you deny them help. That's why it's important to be truthful with confused persons. They can sense deception and insincerity. Once you've acknowledged their mental state, you can assess its severity and start taking constructive measures to deal with it.

Not too long ago confused patients were dealt with by dumping them in back wards where they experienced no mental stimulation and so continued to deteriorate ever faster. Today we deal with confused geriatric patients truthfully and realistically. Mental faculties dim when people are left without daily conversation concerning current events, weather, holidays, and the concerns of living. It's the purpose of R.O. to reorient such people as much as possible; at the very least, to stop any further deterioration.

Begin by assessing the patient. Included in this chapter are two pre-R.O. tests to determine the degree of his confusion and helplessness. When giving the tests, treat the patient courteous-

PRE-R.O. ASSESSMENT I

Patient's Name   Date

Room Number   Doctor

Diagnosis:

	Correct	Incorrect
1. What is your name?		
2. Where are you living?		
3. When is your birthday?		
4. How old are you?		
5. What year is it now?		
6. What is the date today?		
7. What season is it?		
8. What is the next meal?		
9. Do you have a roommate?		
10. What is his/her name?		

What do you like best about living here?

Evaluator's comments:

Evaluator   Date

ly. The questions you must ask may make him feel inadequate, even embarrassed. Hurrying him along will make him more anxious and confused. Let the patient take his time. If he seems to forget the question, restate it gently and tactfully. A calm, friendly, respectful manner will help put him at ease.

24-HOUR REALITY ORIENTATION

Reality orientation goes on 24 hours a day. Any staff member who notices that a patient or resident seems confused immediately tells him where he is and why, who the staff member is, and the time of day. The resident is never allowed to retreat into his confused world. He's told this information first thing in the morning and repeatedly throughout the day. The program is

PRE-R.O. ASSESSMENT II

Patient's Name _____ Date _____

Room Number _____ Doctor _____

Diagnosis: _____
_____
_____
_____

1. Can you use the toilet?
   Without help _____
   With assistance _____
   Completely unable _____
   No response _____

2. Can you bathe yourself?
   Without help _____
   With assistance _____
   Completely unable _____
   No response _____

3. Can you dress yourself?
   Without help _____
   With assistance _____
   Completely unable _____
   No response _____

4. Can you feed yourself?
   Without help _____
   With assistance _____
   Completely unable _____
   No response _____

5. Can you brush your hair daily?
   Without help _____
   With assistance _____
   Completely unable _____
   No response _____

6. Do you attend activities here?
   Without help _____

   How often? _____
   With assistance _____
   How often? _____
   Completely unable _____
   No response _____

7. Can you tell the nurses if you
   need something?
   Without help _____
   With assistance _____
   Completely unable _____
   No response _____

8. Can you write letters and
   make phone calls?
   Without help _____
   With assistance _____
   Completely unable _____
   No response _____

9. Can you walk freely about?
   Without help _____
   With assistance _____
   Completely unable _____
   No response _____

10. Can you attend a religious
    service?
    Without help _____
    With assistance _____
    Completely unable _____
    No response _____

Evaluator's comments: _____
_____
_____
_____

Evaluator _____ Date _____

based on consistency and repetition. If even one staff member fails to follow through, the program won't benefit the patients.

Maintain a calm environment. A confused patient becomes more confused under tension. Tension may be caused by conflicts with staff members or problems between the patient and his family, for example. Only after the conflicts have been resolved and the environment is calm can the patient be reoriented.

Keep to a routine so patients know what to expect. Once someone becomes comfortable in a routine, even minor rearrangements of furniture or his daily schedule may confuse him. If you anticipate any changes in routine, tell the patient about them well ahead of time. As a patient progresses, it can help him to assume responsibility for part or all of his daily routine, if he's physically able. Letting him know he's expected to get himself to the dining room by noon, for example, can give him back some of his independence and increase his self-esteem. But make sure he can really make it on his own; never let him flounder.

Reply clearly and concisely to patient's questions. Always answer a patient courteously. Give enough details to satisfy him. Likewise, when you ask a patient a question, be clear and give him plenty of time to answer.

Avoid unnecessarily loud conversation. Don't raise your voice, and never shout. Loud noises can frighten a geriatric patient and worsen his confusion. Raising your voice does not help a patient who's hard of hearing; all he knows is that someone's yelling at him for no apparent reason. Instead, speak in a firm, confident tone and face the patient. Pronounce words clearly and a little more slowly than normal—don't exaggerate and make faces.

Give patients clear directions. A confused patient will become more confused if asked to go to his room when he has no idea how to find it. Take the time to give him detailed directions. If necessary, take him there yourself. Color-coded units and rooms are ideal for geriatric patients.

Encourage correct orientation. Remind any patient who seems confused of the place, time, day, your name, and even his, if necessary.

Direct patients back to reality. Don't let a patient become more confused than he already is. If he starts to ramble, help him put his thoughts in order. Remind him to speak slowly and clearly.

Help the patient understand what you want him to do. When asking a patient to do an elementary task such as washing his face or combing his hair, don't assume he knows how. Demonstrate the task. Guide his hands through the motions. You may have to do this many times until he relearns the task. A patient, cheerful attitude helps reduce his confusion and anxiety.

Be honest with the patient and respect his dignity. Many times we withold the truth, thinking it will hurt the patient. Being untruthful with a patient, however, only adds to his confusion. If he senses you're being untruthful, he'll become distrustful and difficult to communicate with.

When you ask a patient to complete a task, give him the feeling you assume he will do it. First you must decide whether he's capable of doing what you want to request. Then, by a positive approach and confident manner, give the patient the impression that he can do it. After he's finished, acknowledge his achievement but don't over-praise it. Too much praise can carry the hint that you had expected him to fail.

Be consistent in all your dealings with the patient. This is the keystone of the 24-hour R.O. program. When all staff members use R.O. consistently, many patients will begin or continue to function with minimal assistance and supervision. This will help make your work easier.

Reality orientation is based on the theory that there's a usable portion of the brain even in severely brain-damaged patients. It is a 24-hour-a-day crusade; the return to reality goes on around the clock. The confused person is constantly reminded of where he is, why he's there, who you are, and what you expect of him. This basic information, along with the date and time of day, is repeated over and over again. This can easily be accomplished during basic care of such patients. During their baths, meals, activities, and visits with families and friends, make your statements in a conversational tone. Speak slowly, wait for a reply, and make sure your patients can hear and see you well.

In the following example the italicized words are the clues that orient the patient to his surroundings:

Good *morning, Mr. MacGonigle.* How are you today? (Wait for a reply.) It's a beautiful *fall day.* It must be *40 degrees* already, and it's such a crisp, clear *morning.* Are you ready for your *breakfast?*

(Wait for the patient's reply.) Here's your *breakfast tray.* It's *8 o'clock* in the *morning* and your *breakfast* is here. These *pancakes* look delicious. *Mr. MacGonigle,* would you like *syrup* on your *pancakes?* (Wait for the patient's reply.)

These few sentences remind the confused patient of the time of day, his name, the season, the weather, and what he's supposed to do (eat breakfast). The three questions give him a sense of responsibility. The pauses for his replies reassure him. Conversations like this, no matter how easy they may seem, must be repeated 24 hours a day, seven days a week.

A Federally funded longitudinal study of R.O. at a large private nursing-home complex, Blue Ridge Haven West in Camp Hill, Pa., supported earlier findings that R.O. restores memory significantly (Kohut, 1977). A most welcome secondary result of the study was the decided improvement in communication and cooperation among staff members. Most of the employees participated in preservice and ongoing workshops conducted by the R.O. certified director of staff education.

REALITY ORIENTATION CLASSES

The 24-hour R.O. program at Blue Ridge Haven West is supplemented by regular R.O. classes for patients, taught by an R.O. certified director of staff education. Classes for confused patients are held on several levels geared to individual capabilities and progress. Classroom materials usually include individual calendars, word/letter games, blackboards, felt boards, mock-up clocks, building blocks for coordination and color matching, plastic numbers, and large-piece puzzles. A prominent visual aid is the R.O. bulletin board, which lists the name of the hospital and its location; the current year, month, and day of the week; the next meal; the weather; and other details. It's placed at eye level. For classes that include both ambulatory and wheelchair patients, two R.O. boards, at different heights, may be a good idea. At Blue Ridge Haven West the R.O. bulletin board has been kept up to date by an elderly resident who enjoys helping confused patients and, in turn, feels useful.

The same nursing-home complex also starts the day's activities with a 10:00 A.M. "radio" broadcast over the public-address system (see box).

Classes should be limited to five or six people. This gives each patient more time to talk and allows you to give them more individual attention. A small group is also much easier for a confused person to relate to. The pre-R.O. assessment tests are an excellent tool for evaluating patients' capabilities and selecting class members.

R.O. classes should be held daily for one-half hour. Choose a time when the patients are most relaxed and alert, and schedule the class regularly at that hour. Select a quiet, well-lighted, well-ventilated room, preferably with a door that can be shut to eliminate outside stimulus or noise. The room should have a table for patients to sit around and an area where patients in wheelchairs can form a semicircle in front of the instructor and props. The props for R.O. are inexpensive, ordinary items that can be collected and used on a daily basis:

1. Large clocks
2. Magazines
3. Colorful pictures
4. Posters
5. Maps
6. R.O. bulletin board
7. Day-by-day calendar
8. Games
9. Record player
10. Radio
11. Picture cards
12. Food models
13. Flannel or felt boards
14. Alphabet blocks

The R.O. bulletin board must be used in basic classes. It can be easily made or inexpensively purchased. A flannel or felt board is ideal. It must be easily legible, with a colored background and large letters. It should show the name of the facility, its location, the date, weather, next meal to be served, the next holiday, and other important or current information.

The three steps in an R.O. session are (1) establishing a climate of acceptance, (2) building a bridge to reality, and (3) creating a climate of appreciation. Establish a climate of acceptance by first introducing yourself to each patient. Then introduce the

R.O. RADIO PROGRAM OUTLINE

Good morning. My name is _____.
This is WBRH, the Blue Ridge Haven radio station,
on the air Monday thru Friday at 10:00 A.M.
Today is _____, 1982.
The time is 10:00 A.M.
The weather for today is   _____

_____

The following people are celebrating birthdays today:

_____

_____

Happy birthday to all of you.

The activities schedule for today is (what, when, where):

_____

_____

A special activity for this week is (what, when, where):

_____

Here are some items in the news today:

_____

This is station WBRH signing off until _____ at 10:00 A.M.

patients to each other, one at a time. Don't forget to shake hands; remember the importance of touch. For severely regressed or withdrawn patients, this first step may be enough.

Start building a bridge to reality by asking each patient to read the R.O. board. The board may lead spontaneously to a discussion, or you may want to introduce a special topic or ask class members to read and comment on a simple poem. Keep the proceedings as lively and informal as you can. If patients find the class dull and sterile—or, worse, threatening to their self-esteem—they won't want to return the next day. Encourage them to chat. If someone starts to ramble, steer him back to the subject. Get to know the details of class members' personal lives. The friendlier the environment, the more cooperative the patients will be in their R.O. therapy.

> ### BLUE RIDGE HAVEN WEST
> ### CAMP HILL, PENNSYLVANIA
>
> TODAY IS THURSDAY
>
> THE DATE IS NOVEMBER 18, 1982
>
> THE WEATHER IS SUNNY
>
> THE NEXT HOLIDAY IS THANKSGIVING
>
> THE NEXT MEAL IS LUNCH
>
> TOMORROW IS FRIDAY

The discussion should lead to a climate of appreciation—of self, of each other, or of a poem, for instance. You reinforce this by thanking each group member for attending and by the frequent use of touch.

Before starting each session, make sure all class members are wearing their eyeglasses, hearing aids, dentures, and any other necessary appliances. They can't communicate well if they can't see, hear, or speak clearly. Sit when patients are sitting, in order to be at their eye level. Here's a typical, fairly basic R.O. session:

Instructor: Good morning, everyone. Welcome to your reality orientation class, which meets every day at 10:30 A.M. What a beautiful, sunny, crisp morning! Let's begin by reading the reality orientation bulletin board. Mrs. Hearn, would you like to read the board first?

Patient Mrs. Hearn: This is Blue Ridge Haven West in Camp Hill, Pennsylvania. Today is Thursday, November 18, 1982. The next holiday is Thanksgiving. The next meal is lunch.

Instructor: Thank you, Mrs. Hearn. You read the board very well. Does anyone want to tell us what main dish is served on Thanksgiving Day?

Patient Mrs. Brown: Roast turkey and dressing. I really like roast turkey.

Instructor: It's so good, isn't it, Mrs. Brown? What else did you cook at Thanksgiving?

Mrs. Brown: Sweet potatoes, creamed onions, cranberry sauce, and giblet gravy.

Instructor: That all sounds delicious. I bet you're a good cook! How about adding to the menu, Mrs. Jenkins?

Patient Mrs. Jenkins: (No response.)

Instructor: Mrs. Jenkins, can you name some desserts for the class?

Mrs. Jenkins: (No response.)

Instructor: Can someone name a dessert?

Mrs. Hearn: Pumpkin pie.

Instructor: Good. Mrs. Jenkins, do you like pumpkin pie?

Mrs. Jenkins: Yes—with ice cream.

Instructor: Excellent, pumpkin pie with ice cream. . . . Now let's get back to the R.O. board. Mrs. Jenkins, can you read the board for the class?

Mrs. Jenkins: This is Blue Ridge Haven West in Camp Hill, Pennsylvania. . . .

Instructor: Go on, Mrs. Jenkins.

Mrs. Jenkins: (No response.)

Instructor: I'd like to help you read the R.O. board. . . . Today is Thursday, November 18, 1982. The next holiday is Thanksgiving. The next meal is lunch. . . . Can anyone tell us what the temperature is today?

Patient Mr. Davis: It's cold outside.

Instructor: It's very cold. The temperature is 20 degrees. That's unusually cold for November. Mr. Davis, since it's so cold outside, can you tell us what season it will be in a few more weeks?

Mr. Davis: Winter.

Instructor: That's right; winter will be here December 22. Just about a month away. Well, it's 11 o'clock—time for our class to end. Thank you for coming this morning. Let's all shake hands and say goodbye until tomorrow at 10:30.

In addition to a dialogue such as this, the instructor should always identify her/himself and use touch often during the session, especially in praising a participant who gives a correct answer. Move the class along if one member, like "Mrs. Jenkins," doesn't answer or gives an incorrect reply. Never let an unresponsive patient feel you're putting him on the spot.

The basic class teaching should continue until the patient is ready to progress to a more advanced experience. You can easily evaluate this by the patient's response to his basic environment.

Does he know who he is, where he is, who you are, the date, the time? Is he reaching out to other residents and members of the class? The time for an R.O. patient is as long as he needs. Don't hurry him; be patient. R.O. is usually a long, slow process. The basic R.O. classes can take as little as a week for one person and as long as three or four months for another.

For some, R.O. may not work at all. Dr. James C. Folsom, who pioneered the development of the theory and techniques, states: "Reality Orientation does not work all the time, nor at the same speed, nor to the same degree for every patient. Each patient is different" (Folsom, 1973). But, since stopping regression is also considered success in an R.O. program, it's important not to get discouraged.

More advanced R.O. classes are similar to the basic session. The advanced class meets daily at a regular time for 30 minutes. The R.O. board is reviewed in a more conversational tone, and a higher performance level is expected. Simple crafts can be started and group activities with classmates initiated. The advanced class should be more individualized. The purpose and procedures are the same for advanced classes as for the basic class. Emphasis should still be placed on time, place, and person. The principal props should still be used regularly for continued review and reality orientation.

GUIDELINES FOR CONDUCTING AN R.O. CLASS

1. The R.O. instructor or a resident should prepare the R.O. board and make sure it's up to date and accurate. The classroom should be well lighted and ventilated.
2. Make sure patients are wearing their eyeglasses, hearing aids, dentures, and any other necessary appliances. Sit at eye level.
3. Begin the class by introducing yourself to each patient. Always call the patient by his name and encourage him to call others in the class by their names. Shake hands with each one of the patients and encourage all patients to shake hands with each other.
4. Introduce the class: "This is a class designed to help us remember and to exercise our minds. Class will meet every day for one-half hour at _____."

R.O. PROGRESS REPORT

Resident's Name   Group Number _____

Leader(s) _____   Date _____

	1st	4th	8th	12th	
INTEREST					
	___	___	___	___	Refuses to come to meeting
	___	___	___	___	Attends but shows little interest
	___	___	___	___	Shows some interest
	___	___	___	___	Interested
AWARENESS					
	___	___	___	___	Usually unaware of what is going on
	___	___	___	___	Distracted by voices
	___	___	___	___	Sometimes unaware of what is going on
	___	___	___	___	Usually aware of proceedings
	___	___	___	___	Always aware of proceedings
PARTICIPATION					
	___	___	___	___	Does not talk
	___	___	___	___	Sometimes answers direct questions
	___	___	___	___	Usually answers direct questions
	___	___	___	___	Sometimes volunteers comments
KNOWLEDGE					
	___	___	___	___	Has very little knowledge of average topic
	___	___	___	___	Occasionally answers incorrectly or not on topic
	___	___	___	___	Has good knowledge of average topic

continued

R.O. PROGRESS REPORT (CONTINUED)

Resident's Name _____ Group Number _____

Leader(s) _____ Date _____

	1st	4th	8th	12th	
READING					
	___	___	___	___	Refuses to read
	___	___	___	___	Cannot see to read
	___	___	___	___	Participates
GROUP RELATIONS					
	___	___	___	___	Participates in inter-group comments
	___	___	___	___	Has good relationship with others in group
	___	___	___	___	Does not resent being interrupted
	___	___	___	___	Resents being interrupted
	___	___	___	___	Shy
	___	___	___	___	Interrupts others
	___	___	___	___	Argues with others
	___	___	___	___	Gets angry easily

ENJOYMENT YES ___ SOMETIMES ___ NO ___ Does resident seem to enjoy meetings?

PROGRESS YES ___ NO ___ Since the last report, if any, has resident shown any improvement in meeting? If yes, in what way?

YES ___ NO ___ Since the last report, if any, has resident shown any improvement on the ward?

PLACEMENT

_____ Do you think resident should stay with the same group?

_____ Move to a lower group?

_____ Move to an advanced group?

5. Have each patient read the board. After he successfully reads the information on the board, get him talking about himself, his family, hometown, or former occupation. Be prepared to know all this information so you can recognize and encourage correct responses.

6. A large mock-up-clock may be used in conjunction with a real clock. Set the mock-up clock at the time of the class and ask a patient to read it.

7. Remember that the attention span of these patients is limited. If someone is unresponsive or answers an elementary question incorrectly, make him aware that you appreciate his effort and give him a few clues. But don't drag it out to the point where the other patients get bored or the unresponsive patient feels you're putting pressure on him.

8. Generate stimulating conversation. Here are some simple questions you might ask during a basic R.O. class:
   What season is this?
   What kind of an animal barks, moos, baas?
   What did you have for breakfast today?
   What color is the opposite of black?
   What's your favorite holiday?

9. Establish attainable goals and give reward, praise, and recognition immediately. Face the patient when speaking and touch him when appropriate.

10. Have a disruptive patient removed if he starts to disturb the other class members.

WRITTEN RECORDS

It isn't always necessary to keep written records of patients' progress in an R.O. program. However, progress reports can be very useful in deciding whether to: hospitalize a nursing-home resident, release a patient to his family or a halfway house, or transfer a patient to another group. Written reports can also help a nursing-home director or geriatric-care supervisor in reporting to the members of a patient's family. Finally, written reports make it possible to evaluate the effectiveness of an R.O. group and its leader.

Progress reports should be made at the end of the first, fourth, eighth, and 12th weeks of the program. If the series of

---

R.O. LOG

Class Number

Date Started   Date Ended

Leader(s)

Date   Topics, Activities   Residents Attending (Initials)

Comments:

---

classes is scheduled to end or break after 12 weeks, members of the group should be informed well in advance; after all, that's part of the reality they need to accept. If the series is planned to run continuously, a fresh form can be used for the 16th, 20th, 24th, and 28th weeks, and so on.

It's also helpful to keep an R.O. log that shows the number of residents who attended each day, the discussion topics or activities, and the instructor's comments. Was there a noticeable drop in attendance the day after a certain topic was discussed or a particular activity carried out? If so, the session may have bored, offended, or threatened some patients; better substitute another activity in your future R.O. program plans.

References

Folsom, J. C. "Major Problems in the Treatment of 'Senility.'" Paper presented at the 18th Annual Conference of the Veterans Administration: Studies in Mental Health and Behavioral Sciences, Washington, D.C., March 28–30, 1973.

Kohut, J. J. Unpublished observations, 1977-1982.

12
REMOTIVATION THERAPY

Remotivation therapy is similar to reality orientation and incorporates many aspects of R.O. But there are important differences.

Whereas R.O. is used primarily to help confused geriatric or C.B.S. patients adjust to their surroundings, remotivation is directed more toward withdrawn but still verbal individuals who need stimulation to participate in their environment. Remotivation therapy is an objective technique, used with groups, designed to reach the unwounded areas of the patient's personality and help him want to "live again." The technique was originated by a volunteer in a Veterans Administration hospital. It has gained such wide acceptance that standard courses in it are now taught by certified remotivation trainers who are members of the National Remotivation Technique Organization.

A patient in a nursing home, rehabilitation facility, or mental institution may have access to several kinds of treatment, including occupational, work, rehabilitation, drug, art, music, physical, medical, and psychiatric therapy. Unless he willingly participates in these programs, he can't derive full therapeutic benefit from them. Remotivation therapy provides the extra "push" that can help him participate. With some exceptions, it can be used regardless of the patient's age, illness, or length of institutionalization.

A trained aide or leader meets once or twice a week for about an hour with a small group of patients—no more than 12.

The patients are encouraged, not required, to attend regularly. The leader brings up an objective topic for discussion—current events, natural history, sports, cars, for instance. The leader plans her material according to five specific steps in the remotivation process:

1. Creating a climate of acceptance;
2. Using objective ideas as a bridge to the real world;
3. Sharing the world in which we live;
4. Appreciating the work of the world;
5. Creating a climate of appreciation.

The discussion topic can come from almost any objective—i.e., nonemotional—area of common interest. Choose material you think will interest your patients and that is also familiar to you. Present it at a level the patients can deal with. The discussion topic should be as specific as possible: Instead of the general sport of baseball, get the patients talking about yesterday's game if you know they watched it; instead of "Do you like poetry?" read a short, simple poem or—better—ask one of the group members to do so. Start positively and keep the discussion lively. Bounce simple questions around the group; try to get each patient to answer at least once. Avoid personality clashes among group members, and don't let one or two patients monopolize the discussion.

PROCEDURE

Arrange chairs, including your own, in a circle. Let the patients sit wherever they want in the circle. Start on time and try to keep to the following schedule:

Step 1: Climate of acceptance (5 minutes). Greet patients by name and shake hands. Make any necessary introductions. Get the members to relax with small talk, compliments, and so on.

Step 2: Bridge to the real world (10 to 15 minutes). Bounce questions around the group to warm the members up. Ask questions without "right" or "wrong" answers—for example, where would you like to be? What's your favorite color? Pose only one question at a time. If you can, make the last question lead into the poem or other short passage you've chosen. The poem, in turn, should lead into the main discussion topic.

Step 3: The world we live in (10 to 15 minutes). Use pictures, short articles, slides, or other props to make the topic vivid. Your questions should follow the journalist's *Who? What? How? Where? When?* The objective is to encourage the patients to talk and share their ideas and experiences. Accept whatever the patient has to offer unless it's abusive or off the track. Don't interrupt except to steer a wandering patient back to the topic. Remember: People enjoy talking more than listening.

Step 4: The work of the world (10 to 15 minutes). How does the discussion topic relate to people's daily lives? How do they carry out their jobs? What do they need to know in order to do their work? Would any of the patients in your group like to do this kind of work?

Step 5: Climate of appreciation (5 to 10 minutes). As you thank each patient for attending the session, try to get his reaction to the discussion. If he didn't say much during the session, you can ask him why. Let him know you'd like to hear anything he has to say. As you bid each patient goodbye, remind him of the date of the next session and tell him you look forward to seeing him.

BENEFITS OF REMOTIVATION THERAPY

Remotivation sessions have three important benefits for the patient. They stimulate his mind and help bring him out of the shell into which he has retreated. By actively soliciting his interest in an objective, "real-world" subject, they also help the patient put his personal problems in perspective and keep him in touch with life outside the institution. People in institutions tend to become passive and dependent. Focusing on the real world helps remind them that it's possible and desirable for individuals to take responsibility for their lives, to live freely, and to contribute actively to society. Finally, remotivation therapy gives the patient practice in interacting with others in an atmosphere of acceptance and friendship. Because a "normal" person—the group leader—encourages his participation, his self-esteem is increased.

The hospital or nursing-home personnel who lead remotivation groups benefit from this experience because it can increase their understanding of patients and their problems. Every patient is a person, not just a set of symptoms or a peculiar behavior pattern—a fact that even the most experienced and compassionate nurse or aide can occasionally forget. Bringing an emotionally disturbed person out into the real world, helping him to grow and heal his emotional wounds, is a deeply gratifying experience.

Remotivation groups also help the psychiatric staff. A well-trained leader can do some of the doctor's spadework by stimulating patients' desire for recovery. Her written notes can provide the doctor valuable clues as to patients' vocational and other objective interests.

WRITTEN RECORDS

Paper work is a must. Because the ultimate goal of remotivation therapy is to get the patient out of the institution and functioning constructively as an independent individual, it's vital to keep written records of his progress. The kinds of records vary from institution to institution, but they include individual progress reports and your own log, like the records recommended for reality orientation groups.

WHO CAN BE A GROUP LEADER?

The most important qualification is your own personal interest in helping patients. A warm, understanding attitude, resourcefulness in dealing with unexpected situations (whether a patient suddenly becomes abusive or whether you've just run out of prepared discussion topics, you must be in control of the situation at all times), and willingness to give more than you think you've got are crucial to the program's success. The other vital factor is the approval of the director and nursing supervisor of the facility.

The remotivation program in each facility is under the charge of a coordinator. He or she cooperates with the director and nursing supervisor in selecting trainees and arranging for their instruction, keeps a file of records on the program, helps schedule group sessions, establishes a library of materials for use in the remotivation groups, and acts as spokesperson for the program.

All personnel should receive general orientation in remotivation therapy. As in 24-hour R.O., everyone's cooperation is needed for the program to succeed. One slighting remark or careless treatment from an unthinking staff member can undo weeks of effort.

Nurses or aides who want to become group leaders then take a 10-hour mini-course of detailed instruction and practice. It's better to take the course in-house, but if a regional training center is nearby the course can be taken there. The mini-course is tailored to the facility; it will be different for a nursing home, mental hospital, general hospital, or halfway house, for example.

An advanced 30-hour course is offered to those who have completed the general orientation and 10-hour mini-course. On its completion a certificate is awarded that verifies the graduate as a trainer in remotivation therapy. If you become a certified trainer, any facility in which you're employed may be qualified as a remotivation training center.

The National Remotivation Technique Organization (N.R.T.O.) publishes a Remotivation Information Kit ($3.75 each; *prepaid only*). Specify Nursing Home or Psychiatric Edition when ordering. The N.R.T.O. will also provide, on request, the addresses of facilities in any region of the United States that offer workshops and certificates in remotivation therapy. Information can be obtained from:

National Remotivation Technique Organization
Mr. Clifford Young, Director
Training and Evaluation Center
Philadelphia State Hospital
14000 Roosevelt Boulevard
Philadelphia, Pa. 19114
(215) 671-4939.

13

GOAL PLANNING

Goal planning is a method of helping someone improve performance. For a patient or resident in a nursing home or hospital, the ultimate goal is to live as independently as possible within physical limitations.

An elderly person can still be a whole person. He still has the need to grow and change; he can still thrive on challenge. Deep down, his innate human dignity makes him resent the dependence and passivity that come from playing by the institution's rules—the institutionalization syndrome described in Chapter 7.

Goal planning must actively involve the individual patient or resident. He must cooperate; you can't do it all for him. Therefore, the first step is to help him list his personal strengths and needs.

- Strengths can include what the individual enjoys doing, what he does without being reminded, what he does well, whom he likes and trusts, what he likes (physical, social, spiritual, intellectual activities), and what his achievements have been.
- Needs might be these: to become more independent and self-sufficient, to become more active physically, to exercise his mind by taking up a hobby or other interest, or to become more active socially.

Write down his needs positively—for example, "needs to make more friends," not "doesn't have any friends." The list of strengths should be longer than the list of needs. It's important not to discourage the patient by letting the list of needs get too long; keep it down to three items at most.

The second step is to help the patient plan the methods he'll use to satisfy his needs. Help him state them concretely and positively. For instance, if he's had a mild stroke and has trouble writing but needs to keep in closer touch with his children who live out of state, he'll need physical therapy to help him regain the ability to write letters. Or if he needs to make more friends, he will do so by spending more time in the lounge or solarium and by actively introducing himself to other residents.

Set realistic target dates and distinguish between short- and long-term goals. As in the preceding examples, the patient's short-term goal would be to begin physical therapy by the beginning of next week. The physical therapist or rehabilitation specialist may then be able to give him a realistic idea of when he'll be able to write again and achieve his long-term goal of keeping in closer touch with his children. Similarly, the patient's short-term goal could be to become acquainted with one new person every day for a week; his long-term goal of making more friends would be achieved almost automatically as he spent more time with people he found most compatible.

In order to achieve his goals, the patient must have the help of staff members. Spell out the responsibilities of all concerned and give them copies of the patient's goal plan.

Finally, review the plan periodically with the patient. As he achieves one goal, he can substitute another. In this way he's constantly challenged to grow, change, and keep from sinking into an institutional rut.

APPENDICES

APPENDIX 1

A CONCEPT OF IN-SERVICE EDUCATION IN NURSING HOMES

Definition. In-service education in nursing homes is a systematic and continuing process of providing job-related learning experiences for all personnel responsible for direct and indirect care and services to patients/residents.

Philosophy. The ultimate goal of in-service education in nursing homes is to improve the quality of life among patients/residents. Therefore a philosophy of in-service education in nursing homes reflects a commitment to the following principles:

- All personnel must be offered the opportunity for growth, development, and advancement of knowledge, understanding, and skills to help them improve their on-the-job performance; in-service education provides such opportunities.
- In-service education enables personnel to provide care and services that promote and maintain independent functioning among patients/residents.
- Continued improvement of the quality of in-service education serves the best interests of the nursing home, its personnel, and patients/residents.
- Continued improvement of in-service education requires the active participation of representatives of all levels of personnel responsible for direct and indirect nursing-home care and services.
- In-service education is an integral part of the management process; the quality of its practice is determined by the climate of acceptance, appreciation, and support engendered by attitudes and actions of administrative and supervisory personnel at all levels of nursing-home organization.
- The climate of acceptance and appreciation of the values of in-service education is established through such administrative action as (1) allocating money, time, and other resources to the in-service education program and (2) encouraging all personnel to communicate their ideas and information about in-service education goals and processes.

Components. In-service education encompasses the following four major components:

1. Orientation—to the home's specific objectives, organization, personnel policies, job descriptions, and physical plant in which care and services are provided to patients/residents. This includes ongoing orientation of all personnel to any changes in the nursing home.
2. Skill training—to develop competence related to physical needs of patients/residents, e.g., nursing care, food service, activities of daily living, safety, and application of written procedures for care of persons with acute or chronic illnesses, including rehabilitative and restorative techniques.
3. Continuing education—to build additional competence and integrate interpersonal skills into all aspects of interaction with patients/residents, families, other visitors to the home, personnel from other departments within the home, etc. Continuing education provides new knowledge, understanding, and skills based on findings of research in the physical and behavioral sciences, e.g., new techniques for serving physical, social, emotional, and spiritual needs of aging persons with illnesses or disabilities in institutional settings.
4. Leadership and management development—for selected personnel who show potential for learning and applying new methods of leadership and management; remedial training for personnel in leadership and management positions who show evidence of need for assistance in this area of on-the-job performance.

Process. The in-service education process applies principles of adult education and motivation by:

- Involving trainees in planning and conducting their own learning experiences;
- Building on and making appropriate use of trainees' previous experience and relating this experience to new ways of doing things;
- Providing immediate opportunities to apply new learning to the solution of practical problems; actively involving trainees in evaluating the results of their exposure to the in-service education program.

It is a systematic process that involves application of the following steps:

- Formulating statements of general and specific objectives;
- Gathering information relevant to needs, problems, and objectives; identifying resources that can be useful in serving needs, solving problems, and achieving specific objectives;
- Planning and implementing the program, e.g., scheduling in-service education sessions, using written program plans and lesson plans;
- Evaluating results of the program; modifying it as necessary to serve changing needs, to solve new or unresolved problems, and to achieve original and additional objectives.

Benefits. For the staff, in-service education:

- Promotes understanding and commitment to the goals of the home through orientation programming;
- Provides satisfaction by developing the skills needed to do a good job on a continuing basis;
- Offers additional satisfaction of the universal human desire for growth and development by providing refresher information and training in new skills;
- Gives staff members a chance to grow with their jobs and to take on additional responsibilities, by offering courses in leadership and management development;
- Actively involves staff members in checking on their own levels of performance and in setting higher standards of on-the-job performance;
- Promotes mutual respect for each other's work roles and responsibilities by giving personnel from various disciplines opportunities to exchange ideas and information and to solve problems together.

For the home, in-service education can promote a higher level of patient/resident care and develop a more efficient and loyal staff. The benefits derived from these achievements may include the following:

- An improved public image of the home within the immediate community (and of nursing homes in general);
- A new perception of the nursing home as a laboratory for ana-

lyzing problems and working out practical solutions to the problems of delivering care and services to chronically ill, aging patients/residents;

- The development of a "neutral" environment in which interpersonal and interdepartmental disagreements can be resolved; where it is a problem, staff turnover can be reduced.

Conclusion. In-service education is instrumental in developing human resources needed to provide care and services that satisfy the complex needs of personnel, patients/residents, families, and the community in which a home is located. In-service education is a continuing responsibility shared by administrative and other personnel responsible for the safety and well-being of nursing-home patients/residents.

Adapted, with permission, from Nursing Home Trainer Program NYM/RMP Project No. 20 61-70 A, United Hospital Fund of New York, December 1972. This concept of in-service education in nursing homes was developed by participants and staff of the Nursing Home Trainer Program, a demonstration project conducted by the United Hospital Fund of New York and funded by a grant from the New York Metropolitan/Regional Medical Program.

APPENDIX 2

HUMAN NEEDS

All people—no matter who they are, where they live, or how old they are—have certain needs. How are these needs met in your own life, and how are they met in a nursing home? What important differences do you see, and how would they affect you if you were suddenly placed in a nursing home? Discuss these questions in groups of three or four to give each person a chance to speak.

1. Physiological needs
   a. Hunger
   b. Thirst
   c. Elimination
   d. Health care
   e. Cleanliness
   f. Others
2. Needs related to shelter
   a. Protection from weather
   b. Privacy
   c. Predictable environment
   d. Comfort
   e. Protection of possessions
   f. Access to amenities (telephone, television, etc.)
   g. Access to outdoors
   h. Others
3. Need for love and affection. Each group member should take turns pretending to be paralyzed from the neck down and unable to speak. Her partner should feed her.
   a. What physical boundaries around ourselves do we create under normal social conditions?
   b. Do these boundaries change if we become helpless?
   c. Can drawing back our boundaries express love? How?
   d. Is expression of love and affection proper and beneficial in an institutional setting? When?
4. Sexual needs
   a. Opportunities
   b. Manifestations

    c. Variations among individuals

    d. Attitudes of other people

    e. Is the shoe on the other foot with sexually active elderly people—i.e., are they viewed as rebels and nonconformists, and does this upset us?

5. Social needs

    a. Communication

    b. Sharing

    c. Need to feel needed

    d. Variations among individuals

6. Ego needs

    a. Sense of achievement

    b. Self-esteem

    c. Freedom to risk failure

    d. Others

7. Self-actualization

    a. Personal growth

    b. Making the most of individual talents

    c. Overcoming handicaps

    d. Others

APPENDIX 3

EMPATHY TRAINING

These exercises in empathy training—learning to feel as others do—are meant to be carried out in partnerships within a group. Members should take turns participating in each exercise so that everyone gets a chance to do and be done unto. Everyone should also get a chance to express her reactions to these experiences of sensory, motor, and social deprivation.

SENSORY LOSS

Find out what it's like—

- To have poor sight: cover a pair of eyeglasses with clear plastic wrap and try to read a newspaper.
- To be hard of hearing: stuff cotton in your ears and listen to a radio or someone speaking on the telephone.
- To be arthritic: tape the second knuckles of your hands loosely together and/or tape a ruler to the side of your leg above and below the knee; then try to button a shirt and/or climb stairs.
- To have lost your sense of smell: stuff cotton in your nostrils and eat an apple.
- To have trouble speaking because of stroke or dental problems: repeat the Pledge of Allegiance at normal speed with a hard candy ball in your mouth.
- To have shaky hands: write your name with your nondominant hand.

MOTOR LOSS

These exercises emphasize the elderly patient's dependence on those who care for him.

1. Sit in a wheelchair and chat with other group members. One member or the instructor should abruptly wheel you away in the middle of the conversation, without excusing herself or apologizing.
2. Lie propped up in bed and have your partner feed you a little faster than you can comfortably chew and swallow food or drink.

3. Lie in bed and have your partner tie your hand to the side. Wait alone in the room, with the door closed, until she decides to return.

QUESTIONS FOR GROUP DISCUSSION

1. What were your feelings about yourself during these empathy-training exercises?
2. Did your partner's behavior change? If so, how?
3. Did your attitude toward your partner change? If so, in what way or ways?
4. Did your partner's attitude toward you change? If so, in what way or ways?
5. What can you do to make life more pleasant and comfortable for persons with such handicaps?

- For poor sight: provide good, direct lighting; make sure eyeglasses are clean.
- For hearing loss: make sure hearing aid is in place and working properly; speak clearly, slowly, and directly.
- For stiff joints: help only as much as the patient needs; touch and handle his body gently and tenderly.
- For loss of senses of smell and taste: make sure food is warm, appetizing, and attractively served; make sure dentures are in place and clean; allow a hand-fed patient plenty of time to chew and swallow.
- For slowness in action and response: allow plenty of time; never rush a patient.
- Help patients keep themselves neat, clean, and becomingly dressed; shave men if necessary, and remove facial hair from women; remember mouth, hand, and foot care; encourage patients to wear clean clothes and use deodorant.
- Use reality orientation techniques (Chapter 11) if a patient seems confused.

APPENDIX 4

HELPFUL HINTS TO FRIENDS OF
HARD-OF-HEARING PEOPLE

When talking to the hard-of-hearing person you will be able to help him understand you more clearly if you follow these simple suggestions:

1. Talk at a moderate rate.
2. Keep your voice at about the same volume throughout, without dropping the voice at the end of each sentence.
3. Always speak as clearly and accurately as possible. Consonants, especially, should be articulated with care.
4. Do not "over-articulate"; i.e., mouthing or overdoing articulation is just as bad as mumbling.
5. Pronounce every name with care. Make a reference to the name for easier understanding, as: Joan, "the girl from the office," or Penney's, "the downtown store."
6. Change to a new subject at a slower rate, making sure that the person follows the change. A key word or two at the beginning of a new topic is a good indicator.
7. Do not attempt to converse while you have something in your mouth, such as a pipe, cigar, cigarette, or chewing gum. Do not cover your mouth with your hand.
8. Talk in a normal tone of voice. Shouting does not make your voice more distinct. In some instances shouting makes it more difficult for a hard-of-hearing person to understand.
9. Address the listener directly. Do not turn away in the middle of a remark or story. Make sure that the listener can see your face easily and that a good light is on it.
10. Use longer phrases, which tend to be easier to understand than short ones. For example, "Will you get me a drink of water?" presents much less difficulty than "Will you get me a drink?" Word choice is important here. Fifteen and fifty cents may be confused, but a half dollar is clearer.

Courtesy of the Sacramento Hearing Society, Inc.

APPENDIX 5

A PATIENT'S BILL OF RIGHTS

The American Hospital Association presents a Patient's Bill of Rights with the expectation that observance of these rights will contribute to more effective patient care and greater satisfaction for the patient, his physician, and the hospital organization. Further, the Association presents these rights in the expectation that they will be supported by the hospital on behalf of its patients, as an integral part of the healing process. It is recognized that a personal relationship between the physician and the patient is essential for the provision of proper medical care. The traditional physician-patient relationship takes on a new dimension when care is rendered within an organizational structure. Legal precedent has established that the institution itself also has a responsibility to the patient. It is in recognition of these factors that these rights are affirmed.

1. The patient has the right to considerate and respectful care.
2. The patient has the right to obtain from his physician complete current information concerning his diagnosis, treatment, and prognosis in terms the patient can understand. When it is not medically advisable to give such information to the patient, the information should be made available to an appropriate person in his behalf. He has the right to know, by name, the physician responsible for coordinating his care.
3. The patient has the right to receive from his physician information necessary to give informed consent prior to the start of any procedure and/or treatment. Except in emergencies, such information for informed consent should include but not necessarily be limited to the specific procedure and/or treatment, the medically significant risks involved, and the probable duration of incapacitation. Where medically significant alternatives for care or treatment exist, or when the patient requests information concerning medical alternatives, the patient has the right to such information. The patient also has the right to know the name of the person responsible for the procedures and/or treatment.

4. The patient has the right to refuse treatment to the extent permitted by law and to be informed of the medical consequences of his action.
5. The patient has the right to every consideration of his privacy concerning his own medical care program. Case discussion, consultation, examination, and treatment are confidential and should be conducted discreetly. Those not directly involved in his care must have the permission of the patient to be present.
6. The patient has the right to expect that all communications and records pertaining to his care should be treated as confidential.
7. The patient has the right to expect that within its capacity a hospital must make reasonable response to the request of a patient for services. The hospital must provide evaluation, service, and/or referral as indicated by the urgency of the case. When medically permissible, a patient may be transferred to another facility only after he has received complete information concerning the needs for and alternatives to such a transfer. The institution to which the patient is to be transferred must first have accepted the patient for transfer.
8. The patient has the right to obtain information as to any relationship of his hospital to other health care and educational institutions insofar as his care is concerned. The patient has the right to obtain information as to the existence of any professional relationships among individuals, by name, who are treating him.
9. The patient has the right to be advised if the hospital proposes to engage in or perform human experimentation affecting his care or treatment. The patient has the right to refuse to participate in such research projects.
10. The patient has the right to expect reasonable continuity of care. He has the right to know in advance what appointment times and physicians are available and where. The patient has the right to expect that the hospital will provide a mechanism whereby he is informed by his physician or a delegate of the physician of the patient's continuing health care requirements following discharge.

11. The patient has the right to examine and receive an explanation of his bill regardless of source of payment.
12. The patient has the right to know what hospital rules and regulations apply to his conduct as a patient.

No catalog of rights can guarantee for the patient the kind of treatment he has a right to expect. A hospital has many functions to perform, including the prevention and treatment of disease, the education of both health professionals and patients, and the conduct of clinical research. All these activities must be conducted with an overriding concern for the patient, and, above all, the recognition of his dignity as a human being. Success in achieving this recognition assures success in the defense of the rights of the patient.

APPENDIX 6

CRUSHING TABLETS, OPENING CAPSULES: WHEN IS IT SAFE?

Gilles L. Fraser, Pharm.D.

Swallowing a tablet or capsule ought to be simple, but it can be a difficult undertaking for the elderly. Most of the time these patients—or those who take care of them—can resort to the traditional solution of crushing the tablet or opening the capsule and mixing the medication with fluid or food. But some drugs come in forms that can't be altered without changing therapeutic effect. Among the non-crushable forms are enteric-coated tablets, designed for dissolution in the intestine rather than in the stomach; tablets coated to give both immediate and delayed action; tablets within tablets, usually of different colors, for the same purpose; uncoated tablets speckled with beads for delayed action; uncoated tablets designed to dissolve in the mouth for absorption through the oral mucosa. Capsules containing beads or pellets, usually for delayed action, may be opened and the contents ingested, but only if they are not crushed or chewed. But since this is difficult to assure, it's usually better not to open these capsules.

Even if a tablet can be crushed safely, a liquid formulation of the drug may be available. But remember that liquid formulations are absorbed quickly into the bloodstream, so they can't take the place of prolonged-release tablets.

The following table lists oral drugs and combination products commonly prescribed for the elderly, and tells whether a liquid formulation is available and whether you can safely crush the tablet or open the capsule.

Gilles L. Fraser, Pharm.D., is clinical pharmacist at the Central Maine Medical Center, Lewiston. This table is an updated version of one originally developed by Dr. Fraser in collaboration with Henry A. Palmer, Ph.D., assistant dean for clinical affairs, University of Connecticut School of Pharmacy, Storrs.

Product	Solid formulation	Liquid formulation	May tablet be crushed or capsule opened?
Achromycin (tetracycline)	100-, 250-, 500-mg capsules	125 mg/5 ml	Yes
Actifed	Tablet with 2.5 mg triprolidine, 60 mg pseudoephedrine	1.25 mg triprolidine, 30 mg pseudoephedrine/5 ml	Yes
Adapin (doxepin)	10-, 25-, 50-, 100-mg capsules	None	Yes
Aldactazide	Tablet with 25 mg hydrochlorothiazide, 25 mg spironolactone	None	Yes
Aldactone (spironolactone)	25-, 100-mg tablets	None	Yes
Aldomet (methyldopa)	125-, 250-, 500-mg tablets	None	Yes
Aldoril	Tablets with 15 or 25 mg hydrochlorothiazide, 250 mg methyldopa; 30 or 50 mg hydrochlorothiazide, 500 mg methyldopa	None	Yes
Amcill (ampicillin)	250-, 500-mg capsules; 125-mg chewable tablet	125 mg/5 ml, 250 mg/5 ml	Yes
Amoxil (amoxicillin)	250-, 500-mg capsules	125 mg/5 ml, 250 mg/5 ml	Yes
Antivert (meclizine)	12.5-, 25-mg tablets; 25-mg chewable tablet	None	Yes
Apresoline (hydralazine)	10-, 25-, 50-, 100-mg tablets	None	Yes

Product	Solid formulation	Liquid formulation	May tablet be crushed or capsule opened?
Aristocort (triamcinolone)	1-, 2-, 4-, 8-, 16-mg tablets	2 mg/5 ml	Yes
Artane (trihexyphenidyl)	2-, 5-mg tablets; 5-mg sustained-release capsule	2 mg/5 ml	Yes (tablets) No (capsule)
Asendin (amoxapine)	50-, 100-, 150-mg tablets	None	Yes
Atarax (hydroxyzine)	10-, 25-, 50-, 100-mg tablets	10 mg/5 ml	Yes
Ativan (lorazepam)	0.5-, 1-, 2-mg tablets	None	Yes
Atromid-S (clofibrate)	500-mg capsule	None	Yes*
Aventyl (nortriptyline)	10-, 25-mg capsules	10 mg/5 ml	Yes
Azo Gantrisin	Tablet with 500 mg sulfisoxazole, 50 mg phenazopyridine	None	Yes†
Bactrim	Tablets with 400 mg sulfamethoxazole, 80 mg trimethoprim; 800 mg sulfamethoxazole, 160 mg trimethoprim	200 mg sulfamethoxazole, 40 mg trimethoprim/5 ml	Yes
Benadryl (diphen-hydramine)	25-, 50-mg capsules	12.5 mg/5 ml	Yes
Bentyl (dicyclomine)	10-mg capsule, 20-mg tablet	10 mg/5 ml	Yes

*It may be difficult to extract the contents of the capsule completely.
†May stain teeth if crushed tablet is in prolonged contact with them.

Product	Solid formulation	Liquid formulation	May tablet be crushed or capsule opened?
Bentyl with phenobarbital	Capsule with 10 mg dicyclomine, 15 mg phenobarbital; tablet with 20 mg dicyclomine, 15 mg phenobarbital	10 mg dicyclomine, 15 mg phenobarbital/ 5 ml	Yes
Blocadren (timolol)	10-, 20-mg tablets	None	Yes
Brethine (terbutaline)	2.5-, 5-mg tablets	None	Yes
Butazolidin (phenylbutazone)	100-mg capsule	None	Yes
Butisol Sodium (butabarbital)	15-, 30-, 50-, 100-mg tablets and capsules	30 mg/5 ml	Yes
Calan (verapamil)	80-, 120-mg tablets	None	Yes
Carafate (sucralfate)	1-gm tablet	None	Yes
Cardilate (erythrityl tetranitrate)	5-, 10-, 15-mg tablets; 10-mg chewable tablet	None	Yes
Catapres (clonidine)	0.1-, 0.2-mg tablets	None	Yes
Chlor-Trimeton (chlor-pheniramine)	4-mg tablet; 8-, 12-mg repeat-action tablets	2 mg/5 ml	Yes (4-mg tablet) No (repeat-action tablets)
Cleocin (clindamycin)	75-, 150-mg capsules	75 mg/5 ml	Yes

Product	Solid formulation	Liquid formulation	May tablet be crushed or capsule opened?
Clinoril (sulindac)	150-, 200-mg tablets	None	Yes
Cogentin (benztropine mesylate)	0.5-, 1-, 2-mg tablets	None	Yes
Combid	Sustained-action capsule with 5 mg isopropamide, 10 mg prochlorperazine	None	No
Compazine (prochlor-perazine)	5-, 10-, 25-mg tablets; 10-, 15-, 30-, 75-mg sustained-action capsules	5 mg/5 ml, 10 mg/ml	Yes (tablets) No (capsules)
Corgard (nadolol)	40-, 80-, 120-, 160-mg tablets	None	Yes
Coumadin (warfarin)	2-, 2.5-, 5-, 7.5-, 10-mg tablets	None	Yes
Cyclospasmol (cyclandelate)	100-mg tablet; 200-, 400-mg capsules	None	Yes
Dalmane (flurazepam)	15-, 30-mg capsules	None	Yes
Darvon (propoxyphene)	32-, 65-mg capsules	None	Yes
Demerol (meperidine)	50-, 100-mg tablets	50 mg/5 ml	Yes
Diabinese (chlorpropamide)	100-, 250-mg tablets	None	Yes
Diamox (acetazolamide)	125-, 250-mg tablets; 500-mg sustained-action capsule	None	Yes (tablets) No (capsule)

Product	Solid formulation	Liquid formulation	May tablet be crushed or capsule opened?
Dilantin	30-, 100-mg capsules (phenytoin sodium); 50-mg tablet (phenytoin)	30 mg/5 ml, 125 mg/5 ml (phenytoin)	Yes
Dimetapp	Sustained-release tablet with 12 mg brompheniramine, 15 mg phenylephrine, 15 mg phenylpro-panolamine	4 mg brompheniramine, 5 mg phenylephrine, 5 mg phenylpro-panolamine/5 ml	No
Diupres	Tablet with 250 or 500 mg chlorothiazide, 0.125 mg reserpine	None	Yes
Diuril (chlorothiazide)	250-, 500-mg tablets	250 mg/5 ml	Yes
Donnatal	Tablet and capsule with 16.2 mg phenobarbital, 0.1037 mg hyoscyamine sulfate, 0.0194 mg atropine sulfate, 0.0065 mg hyoscine hydrobromide	Identical combination in 5 ml elixir	Yes
Donnatal Extentabs	Sustained-action tablet with 48.6 mg phenobarbital, 0.3111 mg hyoscyamine sulfate, 0.0582 mg atropine sulfate, 0.0195 mg hyoscine hydrobromide	None	No
Doriden (glutethimide)	500-mg capsule; 250-, 500-mg tablets	None	Yes

Product	Solid formulation	Liquid formulation	May tablet be crushed or capsule opened?
Dulcolax (bisacodyl)	5-mg tablet	None	No
Dyazide	Capsule with 50 mg triamterene, 25 mg hydrochlorothiazide	None	Yes
Dyrenium (triamterene)	50-, 100-mg capsules	None	Yes
Ecotrin (aspirin)	325-mg tablet	None	No
Edecrin (ethacrynic acid)	25-, 50-mg tablets	None	Yes
Elavil (amitriptyline)	10-, 25-, 50-, 75-, 100-, 150-mg tablets	None	Yes
Elixophyllin (theophylline)	100-, 200-mg capsules; 125-, 250-mg sustained-release capsules	80 mg/15 ml	Yes (plain capsules) No (sustained-release capsules)
Empirin with Codeine	Tablet with 325 mg aspirin plus codeine in one of the following strengths: 7.5, 15, 30, 60 mg	None	Yes
E-Mycin (erythromycin)	250-mg enteric-coated tablet	None	No
Enduron (methy-clothiazide)	2.5-, 5-mg tablets	None	Yes

Product	Solid formulation	Liquid formulation	May tablet be crushed or capsule opened?
Equagesic	Tablet with 150 mg meprobamate, 75 mg ethoheptazine, 250 mg aspirin	None	Yes
Equanil (meprobamate)	200-, 400-mg tablets; 400-mg capsule	None	Yes
Erythrocin (erythromycin stearate)	125-, 250-, 500-mg tablets	None	No
Esidrix (hydrochloro-thiazide)	25-, 50-, 100-mg tablets	None	Yes
Etrafon	Tablets with 10 mg amitriptyline, 2 mg perphenazine; 10 mg amitriptyline, 4 mg perphenazine; 25 mg amitriptyline, 2 mg perphenazine; 25 mg amitriptyline, 4 mg perphenazine	None	Yes
Feosol (ferrous sulfate)	325-mg tablet; 250-mg capsule	220 mg/5 ml	No
Fiorinal	Tablet and capsule with 50 mg butalbital, 40 mg caffeine, 200 mg aspirin, 130 mg phenacetin	None	Yes
Flagyl (metronidazole)	250-mg tablet	None	Yes

Product	Solid formulation	Liquid formulation	May tablet be crushed or capsule opened?
Flexeril (cyclo-benzaprine)	10-mg tablet	None	Yes
Gantanol (sulfa-methoxazole)	500-mg, 1-gm tablets	500 mg/5 ml	Yes
Gantrisin (sulfisoxazole)	500-mg tablet	500 mg/5 ml, 1 gm/5 ml	Yes
Haldol (haloperidol)	0.5-, 1-, 2-, 5-, 10-mg tablets	2 mg/ml	Yes
Hydergine	1-mg tablet; 0.5-, 1-mg sublingual tablets	None	Yes (1-mg tablet) No (sublingual tablets)
HydroDIURIL (hydrochloro-thiazide)	25-, 50-, 100-mg tablets	None	Yes
Hydromox (quinethazone)	50-mg tablet	None	Yes
Hydropres	Tablets with 25 or 50 mg hydrochloro-thiazide, 0.125 mg reserpine	None	Yes
Hygroton (chlorthalidone)	25-, 50-, 100-mg tablets	None	Yes
Ilosone (erythromycin)	125-, 250-mg capsules; 500-mg tablet; 125-, 250-mg chewable tablets	125 mg/5 ml, 250 mg/5 ml, 100 mg/ml	Yes

Product	Solid formulation	Liquid formulation	May tablet be crushed or capsule opened?
Inderal (propranolol)	10-, 20-, 40-, 80-mg tablets	None	Yes
Indocin (indomethacin)	25-, 50-mg capsules; 75-mg sustained-release capsule	None	Yes (plain capsules) No (sustained-release capsule)
Ismelin (guanethidine)	10-, 25-mg tablets	None	Yes
Isordil (isosorbide)	10-mg chewable tablet; 5-, 10-, 20-mg tablets; 40-mg sustained-action tablet and capsule; 2.5-, 5-mg sublingual tablets; 40-mg sustained-release capsule and tablet	None	Yes (plain and chewable tablets) No (other forms)
Kantrex (kanamycin)	500-mg capsule	None	Yes
Keflex (cephalexin)	250-, 500-mg capsules; 1-gm tablet	125 mg/5 ml, 250 mg/5 ml	Yes
Lanoxin (digoxin)	0.125-, 0.25-, 0.5-mg tablets	0.05 mg/ml	Yes
Larodopa (levodopa)	100-, 250-, 500-mg tablets and capsules	None	Yes
Larotid (amoxicillin)	250-, 500-mg capsules	125 mg/5 ml, 250 mg/5 ml	Yes
Lasix (furosemide)	20-, 40-, 80-mg tablets	10 mg/ml	Yes

Product	Solid formulation	Liquid formulation	May tablet be crushed or capsule opened?
Librax	Capsule with 2.5 mg clidinium, 5 mg chlordiazepoxide	None	Yes
Librium (chlor- diazepoxide)	5-, 10-, 25-mg capsules	None	Yes
Lidone (molindone)	5-, 10-, 25-mg capsules	None	Yes
Lincocin (lincomycin)	500-mg capsule	250 mg/5 ml	Yes
Lomotil	Tablet with 2.5 mg diphenoxylate, 0.025 mg atropine sulfate	Identical combination in 5 ml liquid	Yes
Lopressor (metoprolol)	50-, 100-mg tablets	None	Yes
Loxitane (loxapine)	5-, 10-, 25-, 50-mg capsules	25 mg/ml	Yes
Macrodantin (nitrofurantoin)	25-, 50-, 100-mg capsules	Furadantin 25 mg/ 5 ml	Yes
Marax	Tablet with 130 mg theophylline, 25 mg ephedrine, 10 mg hydroxyzine	32.5 mg theophylline, 6.25 mg ephedrine, 2.5 mg hydroxyzine/ 5 ml	Yes
Medrol (methyl- prednisolone)	2-, 4-, 8-, 16-, 24-, 32- mg tablets	None	Yes
Mellaril (thioridazine)	10-, 15-, 25-, 50-, 100-, 150-, 200-mg tablets	30 mg/ml, 100 mg/ml	Yes

Product	Solid formulation	Liquid formulation	May tablet be crushed or capsule opened?
Mephyton (phytonadione)	5-mg tablet	None	Yes
Minocin (minocycline)	50-, 100-mg capsules	50 mg/5 ml	Yes
Moban (molindone)	5-, 10-, 25-mg tablets	None	Yes
Motrin (ibuprofen)	300-, 400-, 600-mg tablets	None	Yes
Mysoline (primidone)	50-, 250-mg tablets	250 mg/5 ml	Yes
Nalfon (fenoprofen)	200-, 300-mg capsules; 600-mg tablet	None	Yes
Naprosyn (naproxen)	250-, 375-, 500-mg tablets	None	Yes
Nardil (phenelzine)	15-mg tablet	None	Yes
Navane (thiothixene)	1-, 2-, 5-, 10-, 20-mg capsules	5 mg/ml	Yes
NegGram (nalidixic acid)	250-, 500-mg, 1-gm tablets	250 mg/5 ml	Yes
Nembutal (pentobarbital)	30-, 50-, 100-mg capsules	18.2 mg/5 ml	Yes
Nicolar (niacin)	500-mg tablet	None	Yes
Nitro-Bid (nitroglycerin for oral administration)	2.5-, 6.5-, 9-mg capsules	None	No

Product	Solid formulation	Liquid formulation	May tablet be crushed or capsule opened?
Nizoral (ketoconazole)	200-mg tablet	None	Yes
Noludar (methyprylon)	50-, 200-mg tablets; 300-mg capsule	None	Yes
Norgesic	Tablets with 385 mg aspirin, 30 mg caffeine, 25 mg orphenadrine; 770 mg aspirin, 60 mg caffeine, 50 mg orphenadrine	None	Yes
Norpace (disopyramide)	100-, 150-mg capsules	None	Yes
Norpramin (desipramine)	25-, 50-, 75-, 100-, 150-mg tablets	None	Yes
Omnipen (ampicillin)	250-, 500-mg capsules	125 mg/5 ml, 250 mg/5 ml, 500 mg/5 ml	Yes
Orinase (tolbutamide)	500-mg tablet	None	Yes
Ornade	Sustained-action capsule with 50 mg phenylpropanolamine, 8 mg chlorpheniramine, 2.5 mg isopropamide	None	No
Oxalid (oxyphen-butazone)	100-mg tablet	None	Yes
Pamelor (nortriptyline)	10-, 25-mg capsules	10 mg/5 ml	Yes

Product	Solid formulation	Liquid formulation	May tablet be crushed or capsule opened?
Parafon Forte	Tablet with 300 mg acetaminophen, 250 mg chlorzoxazone	None	Yes
Parnate (tranylcypromine)	10-mg tablet	None	Yes
Pavabid (papaverine)	150-, 300-mg capsules	None	No
SK-Penicillin VK (penicillin V)	250-, 500-mg tablets	125 mg/5 ml, 250 mg/5 ml	Yes
Pentids (penicillin G)	200,000 U (125 mg), 400,000 U (250 mg), 800,000 U (500 mg) tablets	200,000 U (125 mg)/ 5 ml, 400,000 U (250 mg)/5 ml	Yes
Percodan	Tablet with 325 mg aspirin plus 4.5 or 2.25 mg oxycodone hydrochloride and 0.38 or 0.19 mg oxycodone terephthalate	None	Yes
Periactin (cyproheptadine)	4-mg tablet	2 mg/5 ml	Yes
Permitil (fluphenazine)	0.25-, 2.5-, 5-, 10-mg tablets; 1-mg repeat-action tablet	5 mg/ml	Yes (plain tablets) No (repeat-action tablet)
Pertofrane (desipramine)	25-, 50-mg capsules	None	Yes

Product	Solid formulation	Liquid formulation	May tablet be crushed or capsule opened?
Phenaphen/ Codeine	Tablets with 325 mg acetaminophen, and codeine in one of the following strengths: 15, 30, or 60 mg; 650 mg acetaminophen, 30 mg codeine	None	Yes
Phenergan (promethazine)	12.5-, 25-, 50-mg tablets	6.25 mg/5 ml, 25 mg/ 5 ml	Yes
Phenobarbital	15-, 30-, 65-, 100-mg tablets	20 mg/5 ml	Yes
Placidyl (ethchlorvynol)	100-, 200-, 500-, 750- mg capsules	None	Yes
Polaramine (dexchlor- pheniramine)	2-mg tablet; 4-, 6-mg repeat-action tablets	2 mg/5 ml	Yes (plain tablet) No (repeat- action tablets)
Polycillin (ampicillin)	250-, 500-mg capsules	125 mg/5 ml, 250 mg/5 ml, 500 mg/ 5 ml	Yes
Prednisone	2.5-, 5-, 10-, 20-, 50- mg tablets	5 mg/ml	Yes
Premarin (conjugated estrogen)	0.3-, 0.625-, 1.25-, 2.5-mg tablets	None	Yes
Principen (ampicillin)	250-, 500-mg capsules	125 mg/5 ml, 250 mg/5 ml	Yes

Product	Solid formulation	Liquid formulation	May tablet be crushed or capsule opened?
Pro-Banthine (propantheline)	7.5-, 15-mg tablets; 30-mg sustained-release tablet	None	Yes (plain tablets) No (sustained-release tablet)
Procan SR (procainamide)	250-, 500-, 750-mg sustained-release tablets	None	No
Procardia (nifedipine)	10-mg capsule	None	Yes*
Prolixin (fluphenazine)	1-, 2.5-, 5-, 10-mg tablets	2.5 mg/5 ml	Yes
Proloid (thyroid globulin)	¼-, ½-, 1-, 1½-, 2-, 3-, 5-gr tablets	None	Yes
Pronestyl (procainamide)	250-, 375-, 500-mg tablets and capsules	None	Yes
Provera (medroxy-progesterone)	2.5-, 10-mg tablets	None	Yes
Pyridium (phenazo-pyridine)	100-, 200-mg tablets	None	No
Quibron	Capsules with 150 mg theophylline, 90 mg guaifenesin; 300 mg theophylline, 180 mg guaifenesin	150 mg theophylline, 90 mg guaifenesin/ 15 ml	Yes
Reglan (metoclopramide)	10-mg tablet	None	Yes

*It may be difficult to extract the contents of the capsule completely.

Product	Solid formulation	Liquid formulation	May tablet be crushed or capsule opened?
Regroton	Capsule with 25 mg chlorthalidone, 0.125 mg reserpine; 50 mg chlorthalidone, 0.25 mg reserpine	None	Yes
Renese (polythiazide)	1-, 2-, 4-mg tablets	None	Yes
Restoril (temazepam)	15-, 30-mg capsules	None	Yes
Rifadin (rifampin)	300-mg capsule	None	Yes
Ritalin (methyl-phenidate)	5-, 10-, 20-mg tablets	None	Yes
Robitet (tetracycline)	250-, 500-mg capsules	125 mg/5 ml	Yes
Salutensin	Tablets with 25 or 50 mg hydroflumethiazide, 0.125 mg reserpine	None	Yes
Septra	Tablets with 400 mg sulfamethoxazole, 80 mg trimethoprim; 800 mg sulfamethoxazole, 160 mg trimethoprim	200 mg sulfa-methoxazole, 40 mg trimethoprim/5 ml	Yes
Serax (oxazepam)	10-, 15-, 30-mg capsules; 15-mg tablet	None	Yes
Serentil (mesoridazine besylate)	10-, 25-, 50-, 100-mg tablets	25 mg/ml	Yes

Product	Solid formulation	Liquid formulation	May tablet be crushed or capsule opened?
Sinemet	Tablets with 10 mg carbidopa, 100 mg levodopa; 25 mg carbidopa, 100 mg levodopa; 25 mg carbidopa, 250 mg levodopa	None	Yes
Sinequan (doxepin)	10-, 25-, 50-, 75-, 100-, 150-mg capsules	10 mg/ml	Yes
Singlet	Tablet with 40 mg phenylephrine, 8 mg chlorpheniramine, 500 mg acetaminophen	None	No
Slo-Phyllin (theophylline)	100-, 200-mg tablets; 60-, 125-, 250-mg timed-release capsules	80 mg/15 ml	No (tablets) Yes* (capsules)
Slow-K (potassium chloride)	600-mg slow-release tablet	None	No
Sorbitrate (isosorbide)	5-, 10-, 20-mg tablets; 5-, 10-mg chewable tablets; 40-mg sustained-action tablet; 2.5-, 5-mg sublingual tablets	None	Yes (plain and chewable tablets) No (other forms)
Stelazine (trifluoperazine)	1-, 2-, 5-, 10-mg tablets	10 mg/ml	Yes

*Capsules may be opened, and contents mixed with food, but chewing or crushing should be avoided.

132

Product	Solid formulation	Liquid formulation	May tablet be crushed or capsule opened?
Sudafed (pseudo-ephedrine)	30-, 60-mg tablets	30 mg/5 ml	Yes
Suladyne	Tablet with 125 mg sulfamethizole, 125 mg sulfadiazine, 75 mg phenazopyridine	None	Yes*
Sumycin (tetracycline)	250-, 500-mg tablets and capsules	125 mg/5 ml	Yes
Symmetrel (amantadine)	100-mg capsule	50 mg/5 ml	Yes
Synalgos-DC	Capsule with 356.4 mg aspirin, 30 mg caffeine, 16 mg dihydrocodeine, 6.25 mg promethazine	None	Yes
Synthroid (levothyroxine)	0.025-, 0.05-, 0.1-, 0.15-, 0.2-, 0.3-mg tablets	None	Yes
Tagamet (cimetidine)	200-, 300-mg tablets	300 mg/5 ml	Yes
Talwin (pentazocine)	50-mg tablet	None	Yes
Tandearil (oxyphen-butazone)	100-mg tablet	None	Yes
Taractan (chlorprothixene)	10-, 25-, 50-, 100-mg tablets	100 mg/5 ml	Yes

*May stain teeth if crushed tablet is in prolonged contact with them.

133

Product	Solid formulation	Liquid formulation	May tablet be crushed or capsule opened?
Tedral	Tablet with 130 mg theophylline, 24 mg ephedrine, 8 mg phenobarbital	65 mg theophylline, 12 mg ephedrine, 4 mg phenobarbital/5 ml (suspension); 32.5 mg theophylline, 6 mg ephedrine, 2 mg phenobarbital/5 ml (elixir)	Yes
Teldrin (chlor-pheniramine)	8-, 12-mg sustained-action capsules	None	No
Tenormin (atenolol)	50-, 100-mg tablets	None	Yes
Theo-Dur (theophylline)	100-, 200-, 300-mg sustained-action tablets; 50-, 75-, 125-, 200-mg sprinkle sustained-action capsules	None	No (tablets) Yes* (sprinkle capsules)
Thorazine (chlorpromazine)	10-, 25-, 50-, 100-, 200-mg tablets; 30-, 75-, 150-, 200-mg sustained-action capsules	10 mg/5 ml, 30 mg/ ml, 100 mg/ml	Yes (tablets) No (capsules)
Tigan (trimetho-benzamide)	100-, 250-mg capsules	None	Yes
Tofranil (imipramine)	10-, 25-, 50-mg tablets	None	Yes
Tolectin (tolmetin sodium)	200-mg tablet; 400-mg capsule	None	Yes

*Sprinkle capsules may be opened, and contents mixed with food, but chewing or crushing should be avoided.

Product	Solid formulation	Liquid formulation	May tablet be crushed or capsule opened?
Tolinase (tolazamide)	100-, 250-, 500-mg tablets	None	Yes
Tranxene (clorazepate)	3.75-, 7.5-, 15-mg capsules; 11.25-, 22.5-mg single-dose tablets	None	Yes (capsules) No (tablets)
Tremin (trihexyphenidyl)	2-, 5-mg tablets	None	Yes
Triavil	Tablets with 10 mg amitriptyline, 2 mg perphenazine; 10 mg amitriptyline, 4 mg perphenazine; 25 mg amitriptyline, 2 mg perphenazine; 25 mg amitriptyline, 4 mg perphenazine; 50 mg amitriptyline, 4 mg perphenazine	None	Yes
Triclos (triclofos)	75-mg tablet	100 mg/ml	Yes
Tylenol (acetaminophen)	325-, 500-mg tablets; 80-mg chewable tablet	60 mg/0.6 ml, 120 mg/5 ml, 1000 mg/ 30 ml	Yes
Valium (diazepam)	2-, 5-, 10-mg tablets	None	Yes
Vasodilan (isoxsuprine)	10-, 20-mg tablets	None	Yes
V-Cillin K (penicillin)	125-, 250-, 500-mg tablets	125 mg/5 ml, 250 mg/5 ml	Yes
Verstran (prazepam)	10-mg tablet	None	Yes

Product	Solid formulation	Liquid formulation	May tablet be crushed or capsule opened?
Vesprin (triflupromazine)	10-, 25-, 50-mg tablets	50 mg/5 ml	Yes
Vibramycin (doxycycline)	50-, 100-mg capsules	25 mg/5 ml, 50 mg/5 ml	Yes
Vistaril (hydroxyzine)	25-, 50-, 100-mg capsules	25 mg/5 ml	Yes
Vivactil (protriptyline)	5-, 10-mg tablets	None	Yes
Zaroxolyn (metolazone)	2.5-, 5-, 10-mg tablets	None	Yes
Zyloprim (allopurinol)	100-, 300-mg tablets	None	Yes

OTHER TITLES OF RELATED INTEREST FROM MEDICAL ECONOMICS BOOKS

Practical Guide to Geriatric Medication
  Marc Bachinsky, R.Ph., M.S., et al.
  ISBN 0-87489-205-8

Caring for the Disabled Patient: An Illustrated Guide
  Priscilla B. Eldridge, R.P.T.
  ISBN 0-87489-141-8

Managing Sexual Dysfunction: A Basic Guide
  John F. O'Connor, M.D.
  ISBN 0-87489-217-1

Improving Patient Medication Compliance
  Robert T. Weibert, Pharm.D., and Donald A. Dee, R.Ph., M.S.
  ISBN 0-87489-218-X

OTC Handbook: What to Recommend & Why
Second Edition
  Richard Harkness, R.Ph.
  ISBN 0-87489-303-8

Directing Health-Care Volunteers
  Nancy Kieffer
  ISBN 0-87489-203-1

For information, write to:

Medical Economics Books
680 Kinderkamack Road
Oradell, New Jersey 07649